TOUGH TALK

TOUGH TALK

TRUE STORIES OF EAST LONDON HARD MEN

ARTHUR WHITE
&
IAN MCDOWALL

WITH
MILLIE MURRAY

Authentic

First published 2000
This revised edition published 2011 by Authentic Media Limited
Presley Way, Crownhill, Milton Keynes, MK8 0ES
www.authenticmedia.co.uk

17 16 15 14 13 12 11   7 6 5 4 3 2 1

British Library Cataloguing-in-Publication Data

A catalogue record for this book is available from the British
Library.

ISBN 978-1-86024-823-8

Some of the names and places referred to in these stories have
been changed to protect people involved.

Cover design by Paul Airy at DesignLeft (www.designleft.co.uk)
Cover photograph by David Lund
Printed and bound in Great Britain by Cox and Wyman, Reading

This book is dedicated to

Jacqui, Emma and James White,
without whose love and understanding
Arthur wouldn't have been able to
get through the tough times.

Valerie and Bianca McDowall,
and to Ian's mum, sister and brothers
for their love and support.

CONTENTS

Foreword   ix
Introduction   xi

Arthur White
1. Champion of the World   3
2. Coke – The Real Thing!   15
3. Country Club Affair   24
4. Debt Collector   34
5. Fresh Start   45
6. Conflict and Commitment   57
7. Joining Tough Talk   66
8. Living the Life   75

Ian McDowall
1. Pumping it Up   85
2. Jamaica   98
3. Top Touch   108
4. Knock-back   118
5. Dark and Light   129
6. Peace and Turmoil   143
7. The Power of God   152
8. Tough Talk   162

Epilogue   171

FOREWORD

It is now more than 10 years since the publication of the first edition of this *Tough Talk* book. Since then, in addition to copies sold, thousands of copies have been handed out at meetings in churches, schools and colleges and many thousands of copies have been given to prison chaplaincies. As a result, the book has had to be reprinted many times. Many people, particularly prison inmates, have contacted the team to say how reading the book has affected them and has led them to give their lives to Jesus Christ.

Over these years, the lives of Arthur and Ian have changed as they have faced the challenge of living the Christian life in today's culture. Both their stories now include a section on how their lives have changed as they have continued to live with Jesus at the centre. Also during this time, the make-up of the Tough Talk team has changed and Steve Johnson is no longer part of the group, so his story is not included in this edition.

I have had the privilege of working with Arthur and Ian since 2001 as the team administrator and Chairman of Trustees. As a result, I can assure readers of this book that not only do they 'talk the talk' but really do 'walk the walk' with Jesus Christ and are great ambassadors for him.

I recommend this new edition of *Tough Talk* as a great source of encouragement for Christians and as a powerful evangelistic tool for reaching out to those who desperately need to come to faith in Jesus Christ.

Professor Michael Steward,
Chairman of Trustees of Tough Talk

INTRODUCTION

Since 1995 a group of men from London's East End with backgrounds of bodybuilding and powerlifting have been visiting prisons, schools and churches performing powerlifting demonstrations as a backdrop to sharing their life stories – challenging stories of how their lives were dramatically transformed.

In the year 2000 a book was published which told the stories of three members of the group: Arthur White, Steve Johnson and me (Ian McDowall). The book was entitled *Tough Talk* and the group subsequently formed a registered charity under the same name.

The Tough Talk team is still going strong but since the book was originally published a lot has happened, and Steve Johnson no longer travels with the team, so the stories need to be brought up to date. Using the original accounts, Arthur and I met once again with Millie Murray and developed and expanded our stories.

Tough Talk has affected many people's lives and here are just a few extracts from of some of the letters the team have received:

HMP Highpoint

'You have opened up a new light in my life. After reading your book . . . tears of joy and thankfulness that Jesus has touched your lives were streaming down my face . . .'

HMP Feltham

'I'm James. I've read you book and was overwhelmed by the changes in the men's lives. I'm on remand in Feltham . . . Can God still forgive me of my actions?

HMP Bedford

'I did enjoy reading your book . . . it has made me look at my life, and I know that I cannot be like I am for the rest of my life; I too can be a decent helpful person. I want to be like that, full stop. The book has made me think of a better future.'

HMP Onley

'I've messed up . . . I have a drug problem, I've lost of lost all my friends . . . I want to change my life like Arthur and Ian from Tough Talk . . .'

We receive letters every week from people who have had their life impacted through this book and pray that it will have an impact on your life, too.

Ian McDowall

ARTHUR WHITE

1

CHAMPION OF THE WORLD

'Ladies and gentlemen, the European and World Heavyweight Champion of 1992, from Great Britain, Arthur White!'

The applause was deafening. Walking towards the rostrum with the sound of the crowd in my ears, I felt myself swelling up with pride, ready to burst. As I drew alongside the MC, out of the corner of my mouth, I said to him, 'Would yer say that again?'

'Ladies and gentlemen, the . . .'

His words puffed me up even more. By the time I reached the rostrum I felt that I had added ten foot to my six foot frame. This was what life was all about for me: winning – coming first.

Swaggering across the platform, I raised my hand to acknowledge my followers who were still clapping. Up on the rostrum the applause sounded like thunder. I lifted my hands and turned from side to side. Bright flashes from photographers and the lights from TV cameras boosted my ego even more. This was the 'ultimate' for me; the pinnacle of my sixteen years as an international athlete. I bent my head to receive the medal that Keiron Stanley, President of the British Powerlifting Organisation, placed over my head. In fact, that evening I picked up five medals: European Champion, European Best Lifter, World Champion, runner-up World Best Lifter and British Powerlifting Hall of Fame.

After the awards ceremony I was still riding high from the whole day's events. People came up to congratulate me, slapping me on the back and shaking my hand.

'Well done, mate.'

'Good lifting.'

'I knew yer'd win.'

'Still the best!'

The T-shirt that I was wearing confirmed what had happened to me that night, and what my fans were saying, 'There Can Be Only One'. I wanted the evening to go on forever. A few of the lifters and some of the boys decided to meet up later.

To get out of the forum took ages. It seemed as though people were popping up all over the place just to have a few words with me and to get my autograph. I savoured all the adulation, but I needed to get back to my hotel room. Eventually I managed to manoeuvre myself out of the door. With the crowds behind me, I could now focus on the evening ahead.

My mood was slowly shifting downwards. I knew what was happening – and I knew how to remedy it. As soon as I set foot into my hotel room, I made a beeline for the bathroom. On the shelf was my wash bag. Quickly unzipping it, I pulled out a small paper envelope. My heart began to beat faster as I greedily but carefully unfolded the paper. Throwing the wash bag to one side, I emptied the gram of cocaine onto the glass shelf in a straight line. I then rolled the envelope up and used it as a straw to snort up the powder. The initial feeling of relief was soon followed by a surge of adrenaline pumping through my veins. By the time I got under the shower I felt that I was invincible. It felt as though there was some-body else on the inside of me who wanted to come out. Every fibre of my being was pulsating. I couldn't keep still – I had to get out. Within the space of about five min-utes, I was washed, dressed and out the door, looking for more action.

In the foyer I met up with some of the other guys, and as the cabs came rolling up to the front door we took it in turns to pile in. The effects of the cocaine were really kicking in. My mouth was going nineteen to the dozen. It was a tight squeeze with four other lifters in the cab. I couldn't keep still. I was eager to get to the nightclub.

I didn't have a clue as to where we were going or what the club was called, but as the cab drew up outside, I felt my mood swing up. The bright lights and the crowd of people hanging about outside made me impa-tient to get in.

The atmosphere inside the club was intoxicating. I had brought some more coke with me, just in case. The heavy rhythmic beat captivated my senses. I felt as though the whole of me was taken over by a force, which I wasn't fighting – in fact I was quite happy to be led by the coke, the beer and the hypnotic effects of the club. I couldn't really hear myself think, and to be truth-ful I didn't want to think about my life and what was reality. The here and now was what I was living for.

The music had me swinging my 16½-stone bulk all over the place – John Travolta had nothing on me that night! There were some young dancers up on the podi-ums giving it all they had. My mates and I were laugh-ing at them. Then one of my friends said, "Ere Arfer, you can do better than that.' Grinning, I didn't need to be asked twice. I tore off my jacket, also ripping off my shirt in my haste to get up there. The guy whose spot I took didn't have time to register what was happening to him. I just pushed him out of the way and got down into some serious movements. I thought I was on *Top of the Pops*! I danced non-stop for a while and I would have continued, had the doorman not come along and told me to get down. I knew that I could have easily sorted him out, but it wasn't worth it. I was out for a good time, not for trouble. Anyway, no one could beat me, so I thought it was time for another beer.

The night rushed by all too quickly. Before I knew it, it was time to go. I could have stayed for much longer, but the other guys wanted to go back to the hotel, so we left.

Back in my room, the miserable reality of my life caught up with me. The curtains were drawn and the bedside lamp cast an eerie glow which matched my mood. The coke and booze had worn off; the mask that I had upheld throughout the day was gone. This was the real me. The nightmare that I was living had now come back to haunt me. Sitting in the armchair, I held my head in my hands and wept. This should have been a time of celebration. My wife and kids should have been with me, sharing in my victory. Instead, I was a broken mess. My hard, steel-like exterior was just a façade. Inside I was a lonely man.

Empty of drugs, my mind whirled and somersaulted over different times in my life: at home with my wife, Jacqui, having a meal; in the garden laughing and joking, playing around with my two kids, Emma and James. It all seemed so unreal now; I was miles and miles apart from them – not only in distance but in love, in everyday contact. Resting my head back against the armchair, I wondered what my life was all about.

Tears streamed from my eyes, blurring my vision. The pain of my sobbing was cutting into every part of me.

My chest felt sore with all the heaving and emotional pain that I was experiencing. Now would be the time, I thought, to end it all. No more pain for my wife and kids, and I, too, would be free from this suffering.

Bending down, I unstrapped the twelve-inch diver's knife from my left leg. I rested it on the small table in front of me. The black-handled, shiny silver knife seemed to draw me closer; something was pulling my hand to pick it up. It would be so simple – one slash across my throat – the end.

Beads of sweat trickled down my forehead. The air felt oppressive; I found it difficult to breathe. One cut. Quick. Painless. My eyelids were like sheets of lead. I was perspiring all over. My mind was spinning around like a carousel, out of control. Then it went blank. I felt myself falling into oblivion . . .

The next thing I knew, the pale November morning light was streaming through a gap in the curtains. I felt groggy; it was an effort for me to get up. I began to focus as I stretched my body. My muscles ached. My brain ached. Gingerly, I walked over to the patch of floor where I had thrown my jacket the night before. I fished the small envelope out and started to prepare myself for another rush.

♦ ♦ ♦

Mr Sethers, the PE teacher at Fairmead Secondary School, had told the fourth form class that if anyone wanted to be selected for the school athletics team they had to stay after school for the trials. I didn't have to be asked twice. At 14, I enjoyed sport more than anything. My speciality was sprinting. I had represented the school on a few occasions and was keen to do so again.

Mr Sethers had a bit of a soft spot for me. He was always encouraging me to do better, which boosted my confidence and increased my competitiveness. Wanting to do well in whatever I did, especially sports, was something that I think I must have been born with.

With my hands on the white line and my feet on the starting block, I was poised, ready to shoot off towards the winning line. I won the 100 metres. I usually did. I went on to become the West Essex Junior Champion, Essex Junior Champion, and I equalled the 100 metres national record, all before I was 16.

Living on the Debden council estate in Loughton, Essex, was great for a boy like me. The sprawling estate was surrounded by acres and acres of grass verges, fields, and it bordered Epping Forest. To be able to take a short walk from my house and find myself in a chest-high field of corn was heaven for me. In those days, it was safe for children to go out alone without fear of being abducted, and it was a stark contrast to the war-torn East End I knew as a young child.

At home, my dad was the head of the house. But it was my mum that I shared my innermost thoughts with. She was the one who supported me in all that I did.

It was around this time that I started to train with weights. At first it was just because I wanted to build up more muscle for running, but as my body developed and I felt good about myself, I decided to leave the running behind, and stick with the weightlifting.

Not only was I aware of my body changing, but I also began to pay attention to the opposite sex. I met Jacqui, who later became my wife, when we were both 14 years old. The first time I clapped eyes on her I knew she was the one for me. I was sitting on the wall of a pub – The Gunmakers, in Loughton – when I saw her. My heart skipped a beat and I suddenly felt shy. I would have married her then if I could, but I was prepared to bide my time.

I left school in 1968. At 17, I felt that I could conquer the world. I was eager to earn money, and was confident that I was going to be successful at whatever I turned my hand to. In fact, as I was very good with my hands I became an apprentice carpenter and joiner. C.S. Foster & Sons was a great firm to work for; I came into my own once I started working for them. Being the youngest there, I was taken under the wing of the older men and shown the ropes. I grew up quickly, learning much about both working skills, and life.

By 1972 I was fully qualified and I felt able to face the world and all that it had to offer. Jacqui and I had married the previous year. Life for me was good – I had become a man. It was a great feeling and my desire to be in control of every area of my life propelled me into becoming self-employed. Although I loved working with other people, the time had come for me to branch out on my own.

Any feelings of apprehension that I had about starting up my own business were soon quelled. The building industry was booming. Money was not in short supply. I was prepared to work hard, and it didn't go unnoticed. Soon contracts were coming in from all over the place. I was working from morning to night – I had to. I reasoned to myself that I had to make as much money as I could while I had my health and strength. I had picked the right woman to be my wife, because Jacqui wasn't just my partner at home, she worked right alongside me in the business too. We were very close.

My love for Jacqui grew daily. She was like a part of my body – we thought alike; we were inseparable. I couldn't envisage us ever being apart. When friends or workmates talked about women other than their wives or whistled at women walking past, I didn't join in. I couldn't imagine ever wanting to be with another woman.

During these early years of my working life, for leisure I would go to the gym. This was purely for my own pleasure. I loved training; it was a good way of winding down. There, I was free from the pressures of life. It was a time to clear my mind and help keep my body fit and strong.

Wag Bennett's gym was very popular and well-known. It was frequented by top bodybuilders from all over the world. The actor Arnold Schwarzenegger was a friend of Wag's and a regular visitor.

I loved preening myself in the mirrors around the gym walls. My body was shaping up nicely. The strength that I was gaining was not just superficial muscle. I had tendon strength, which is innate. It's a strength that cannot be acquired – you either have it or you don't. My skeletal frame was also strong, and this enabled me to carry the extra weight.

Deep within myself I also *knew* that I was strong. I created scenarios in my mind where I was battling against the odds, being involved in a train crash where I would not only survive but be a human crane, lifting up the wreckage to save people's lives. Or I would be involved in a horrific car accident and my body would be pierced by a long piece of metal but I would yank it out and, to the amazement of those around me, get up and walk away. I had convinced myself that I was invincible.

At about this time, I met up with a guy called George Manners. He used the gym and was also a coach at the Bethnal Green Weightlifting Club. George invited me to join his club. He had been watching me over a period of time as I trained, and felt that I had something to offer.

At the Bethnal Green club I felt that I had come home. Most of my family originated from east London, and training with the guys there was like being among my family. George was my mentor, and he was a disciplinarian. He had taken part in the 1964 Olympics and had won many competitions. He taught me the correct procedures for weightlifting, and how to discipline myself. He worked me very hard, but it was something that I really enjoyed. He could see that I was eager, and in 1975 he encouraged me to become an instructor.

The instructor's course was being held at the British National Sport Centre at Bisham Abbey in Buckinghamshire, which is where all the England squads train. Whilst there, I met up with Ron Reeves. He owned a gym in Sittingbourne, Kent and had his own team of weightlifters that competed in competitions around the country. He asked me whether I fancied lifting for him at the weekends.

Entering competitions had never really been one of my goals. I was more comfortable with the idea of instructing, but when Ron asked me I considered his proposition. He had obviously been watching me during the weekend and felt that I would be an asset to the team. It didn't take me long to make up my mind to give it a go. I knew I was strong and could handle it, so I told him I would.

I lifted weights for Ron's team from 1975 until 1979. During this time I had a number of successes. I won the Kent Championships three years running, the South East Counties Championships, the Home Counties Championships, bronze medal in the British Championships and bronze medal in the World Championships (which were held in the USA). During this period I also broke a number of British, European and Commonwealth records, and continued to win many smaller domestic competitions.

After six years of marriage, my beautiful daughter, Emma, was born. Jacqui and I had not really thought about having children, we were having such a good time with each other and with our individual interests, but having Emma was a bonus!

My business continued to grow, reaching new heights all the time. In 1980, my son and heir, James, was born and this was truly the 'icing on the cake' for Jacqui and me – our family felt complete.

Although I was having the time of my life, I knew that life for my wife was hard now. She had two small children to look after, as well as running the house. Jacqui still found time to help me as much as she could with the business, and she fully supported me in my weightlifting career. It was difficult for her, but as the children grew up, Jacqui eventually had more time to do the things she wanted to do.

In 1980, I gained a silver medal in the European Championships, second place at the British Championships and a bronze medal at the World Championships. Then in 1981, I kicked off big-time. I was now a regular member of the British Team. I was representing Britain all over the world: USA, Italy, Switzerland, Finland, Germany, India, Holland and France. I felt as though I had become an international globetrotter. Wherever I went I was treated like a celebrity. My entering a competition caused my competitors to fear. They knew that I would be on form and that my one intention was to win a gold, silver, or bronze medal at least. I was no time waster! The adoration that I received made me feel powerful. I felt more than human – bordering on superhuman.

Coming home brought me back down to earth. Initially, having my photo in the papers, attending parties and riding on the wave of my successes was great.

But soon, reality hit home. Back to work, paying the bills, being a loving husband and father and training at the gym sobered me up. Yet, my hankering after the trappings of success grew and grew. It was as though a beast had awakened within me that had to be fed – its food was winning.

I won the 1981 British Championships, the European Championships and I came second in the World Championships. I continued breaking records along the way. I was a force to be reckoned with – nothing could stop me.

In 1982, business was booming and I met a man who was chairman of a group of companies. He gave me a big contract to convert warehouses and offices in Harlow, and it made sense for me to move my whole business there. My dreams and ambitions were literally being fulfilled. I was a walking testament of a man who had everything materially. I didn't want to be king and I had no desire to be the prime minister, but the things that I had attained fulfilled me – nothing seemed to be lacking in my life.

As a member of the British Team, I had to have regular routine medical check-ups. The check-up at this particular time brought a shock for me. The doctor discovered a growth in the back of my throat. I needed an operation straight away. If I continued to lift, it could cause the growth to burst. I didn't want to think about the possible repercussions of such an event. The problem was that I was supposed to be competing in the British Championships in two days – I had to be there to defend my title. I thought about it for a moment. I decided to go to the competition, and I won it. The operation took place the next day and that, too, was successful. A fleeting thought passed through my mind at this time: Was I someone who couldn't be touched by human weakness, or was I a mere mortal? The appearance of the growth, and the subsequent removal of it, had dented my armour. I shook the thought off, and bounced back to normal.

The pressure of work built up. It required more time and effort and so my competing had to be put on hold. I had to apply myself to my work as, otherwise, it would have got out of control – and if I wasn't taking care of it, who would?

The years sped by. I continued to push myself, even though I was not training for a championship. Training was my time for 'me' and I thoroughly enjoyed it.

In 1985, I decided that it was time to start lifting again. I notified the British authorities that I wanted to compete again and they put me straight back on the team, without me having to prove to them my fitness and strength. My reputation preceded me. I was chosen to go and compete in Holland, but I was disappointed in my performance. I came third, when I'd had high hopes of doing much better. My intention, as always, had been to win. This was the second dent in my self-made armour.

2

COKE – THE REAL THING!

'He's gone,' said Frank.

I was confused. 'What d'ya mean, he's gone? What, me dad's up and left? He can't have done, he's 63. Does me mum know where he is?'

It was the early hours of Sunday 11 August 1985. Jacqui and I had only just come home from a fortieth birthday party. The phone had rung as soon as we came through the door.

There was silence at the other end of the line. Then Frank, my parents' neighbour, spoke again. 'Your old man's dead.'

My mind went numb. I mumbled something into the receiver. Then I told Jacqui what had happened. She was just putting James, our son, to bed. Emma was spending the weekend with our neighbours and their children in a caravan. Jacqui, shocked, got James dressed again, and we set off to see my mum.

It wasn't long before we arrived at my parents' place. All the lights were on in the house. My mum was sitting in the front room opposite my dad, staring at him through unblinking eyes. Dad just looked as though he was asleep. His legs were crossed and his head was on his chest. He still had his glasses on. Tentatively, I walked towards him and kissed his cheek. Picking up his cardigan, I draped it over his body.

Tears were flowing down Mum's face. I sat next to her, putting my arm around her shoulders. There was nothing that I could say, or wanted to say. We sat close together for a while, linked by blood and by our pain.

The doorbell rang. It was my eldest brother, Eddie; his face was white.

He stood over Dad. 'Is he dead?'

'Yeah, he is,' I said, nodding.

'No, I mean, is he *really* dead?'

'Yeah.'

I knew what he meant. It looked as though if we had prodded Dad he would have woken up. It just didn't seem real that he was gone. The ambulance turned up soon after, followed by the rest of the family. Once Dad had been taken away, we all sat together making plans for his funeral.

◆   ◆   ◆

Back at work, the sense of losing Dad was strong. In the last few years of my dad's life we had become very close. We were mates, as well as father and son. He had worked for many years as a security guard for a firm of stockbrokers, but had retired due to ill health. Dad then found that he had too much time on his hands, so he had come to work for me. All my workers knew him – he was the type of person that once you'd met him, you never forgot him. His loss was felt by all.

My own sense of mortality was heightened by Dad's death. I had no power (and neither has anyone else on earth) to prevent someone's death. All the money that I possessed couldn't bring Dad back. Death is *final*. Never before, in such depth, had I confronted the extinguishing of life. The truth was, I had subconsciously assumed that I was going to live forever. Once when I lifted 66 stone the power that surged through me caused me to not only feel superhuman, but made me feel that I could never die.

Insidiously, the fear of dying began to come upon me. It was like a black cloak that slowly wrapped itself around my mind. As the days turned into weeks and the weeks became months, I found myself swinging in and out of dark, morbid moods. At times, it was hard to shake them off. Sometimes the periods of depression were so tangible that it was like having another person inside of me.

Taking steroids exacerbated the problem. I was first prescribed steroids for a hip injury. The rapid healing that took place through taking them made me realize how powerful they were. I noticed how quickly my body recuperated after a strenuous bout of training. I progressed from taking steroids in tablet form to injecting them. Unfortunately, the steroids didn't help my state of mind; in fact they made my bad moods worse. The black periods of my life seemed to become more prevalent. Amphetamines helped me a lot; my mood upon waking in the mornings told me what frame of mind I could be in for the rest of the day. I changed that by popping a few pills. But after a while, even the amphetamines didn't help and I was introduced to cocaine.

Coke was surely the 'real thing'. The buzz that I got from it was instant. When I was 'down in the dumps', thinking about life and what it was all about – whether life was worth living, and everything negative – I would snort some coke, and bingo, I would be riding high, soaring through the skies of my mind; nothing and no one could touch me.

Getting my supply of drugs had never been a problem. The crowd of lifters that I was involved with also dealt in drugs. The supply was endless. Huge quantities came across from the continent, and through other channels. But the finance that was needed – about £200 per week – to keep me in drugs was wearing hard on my business. I was still turning over a good profit, but with a house in Loughton and another one in Spain, plus my family to support, I needed to look for another avenue of income. I needed ready, hard cash.

Mickey (one of the guys that I trained with) and I used to have a laugh together. I knew that he didn't have a regular job, and I wondered how he managed to keep his life together.

'Door work, Arfer.'

It didn't appeal to me. Standing outside some nightclub for five or six hours didn't seem like a good way to earn some dough. But the need for drugs exceeded any prejudice I had about being a bouncer. Within a short space of time, I found myself working on the door at the Country Club in Epping, Charlie Chan's in Walthamstow and Mr T's in Erith, earning from £50 to £100 a night.

The glamour of the nightclub scene began to affect me too. The whole atmosphere – the music, the sight of everyone dressed up, and the heady aroma of aftershave and perfume was intoxicating. I had never experienced this type of life before. I wanted more and more. It made me realize that up until that point I had been very naïve to the ways of the world. Yes, I'd done business deals. Yes, I had a wife and children to support. But the darker side of life – wheeling and dealing, drugs – was new to me.

The highlight of any week would be to do a job at an illegal rave. These were mainly held in Barking, north-east

London, usually on a Saturday night. More than eight thousand people would turn up at any one time to a rave. People would start coming from about 9 p.m. and they would dance and freak out to the music until 7 a.m. the next morning. The reason that they were able to keep it up was because most of them were high on drugs.

As doormen, it was our job to body-search everyone that came onto the premises. This netted us a good booty of drugs for ourselves. When the rave was over, we would divide the spoil. The pay for a night's work was the best I ever got, anywhere – £300 to £400. All round, it was a fantastic night out.

Business was still good, but I was feeling restless. No longer did I feel like 'me'. Since I had started to heavily indulge in drugs and had become a doorman, my mind and my lifestyle had become split into different compartments. Dr Jekyll and Mr Hyde didn't have a thing on me! At home I was the dutiful husband and father. It wasn't hard for me to maintain this role, as I still loved my wife and kids very much. But once I donned my persona as a doorman, my personality underwent a change. Wearing the dinner jacket, which was part of my uniform, I felt as if I was ready for any challenge that came my way. I could sense the violence within me building up: it hovered just under the surface of my emotions. I was able to control it – just about. Outside the nightclub doors, my eyes scanned every punter, watching and waiting for something to happen. When it did, I was ready. I would pounce like a tiger, seeking the core of the trouble, picking off the source and overwhelming the person with my now unleashed, violent strength. I never failed.

Still, keeping up appearances was beginning to wear me out. I wanted to remain a doorman; it was my regular business that I was concerned about.

In 1987 there were a lot of changes for me. During the course of my door work, I met a guy called Danny who owned a large building company. We got talking and he handed me his business card.

'If ever you want some work, give me a call.'

I toyed with his proposal. Maybe this could be my way out. The responsibility of running my own business was getting on my nerves. Having to keep things ticking over was getting too much for me. The job offer seemed very appealing, so I called Danny.

'It's all yours, Arfer.'

I didn't have to be told twice. I wound my business up, much to the annoyance of some of my men. But I was only thinking about me – I didn't care about them.

My new job, as a contracts manager, not only paid a good wage but I got a company car too. They also offered Jacqui a job in their offices. So in a way, we were still working together. And without the pressure of running my own business, I decided that now would be a good time for me to do some more competing. Being a life member of the British Amateur Weightlifting Association (BAWLA), I was eligible to compete as long as I made the qualifying lifts, which I was confident I could do.

The 1987 British Championships were held in Milton Keynes. The last time I had been on a British platform I had won. My confidence was high; I was sure that once again, I was going to become a gold medallist. But I was beaten by Johnny Neighbour who wasn't even in my class. In fact, he just wasn't on my level of achievement – and yet this man beat me; he blew me away. I was left reeling in shock at the outcome. Receiving the silver medal didn't placate me.

Later in the year, I was picked to lift for Great Britain in the World Championships in Norway. I gained second place, which I was happy with. But the shadow of my loss at the British Championships was still like a cloud hanging over my head. My confidence had taken a whipping. Johnny Neighbour, through his win, had gone up a class, and he went on to win the World Title.

My determination to win increased. Never again did I want to experience the negative emotions that I did in losing out to Johnny. I trained harder – as far as I was concerned, that was the answer. Looking around me, I noticed the effects of drug-taking in my fellow competitors. The drugs were becoming more scientific and sophisticated; the market was being flooded with them. There seemed to be a limitless supply from both the medical and the veterinary professions. (The drugs that were used on horses and cows were coarser and had a greater impact on human beings.) Whenever these drugs were available, everyone wanted them – they were in high demand. My supplier was excellent; he knew how to get hold of them. It was just like purchasing confectionery.

The more steroids I consumed, the more it seemed that the effect of the amphetamines decreased, so I stopped taking them. But my appetite for cocaine increased tenfold. I couldn't get enough of the stuff. It was very convenient that I worked the doors of nightclubs, because it made getting hold of coke that much easier. I was spending a couple of hundred quid a week fuelling my habit. Sometimes, depending on what was happening in my life at the time, I was spending even more. Coke became a way of life. It was used as a form of currency. My reputation caused it to fall into my life like snowflakes; people, it seemed, wanted to be seen with a celebrity – me. Lines of coke were constantly on offer, and I never refused.

The amazing thing was that my wife never knew what I was up to. She was aware that I was using steroids because of an old injury, but had no idea how much I was taking. Jacqui put my personality changes down to my work. Having two jobs, she assumed, would stress anyone – plus I was training hard too. Her ignorance worked in my favour. Coke is a subtle evil; it crept up on me insidiously, like smog, enveloping me until I was completely immersed. I now needed coke to get through the day.

I had had an on and off relationship with the Epping Forest Country Club. The club was very popular in the Essex area. It was extremely fashionable, and the clientele would come from far and wide to dance the night away. I used to work the door, now and again, but it wasn't until mid 1987 that I had a sort of permanent job there.

Donna was the receptionist at the club when I first started; she was sixteen years my junior. We started off just having the occasional conversation. I was flattered that she wanted to talk with me. She was five foot eight and a size ten, with legs that went on forever. Her long blonde hair was dead straight, and glossy, and her face was always made up to perfection – she was beautiful. She was the sort of woman that if I were younger and free, I would have made it my business to go after. Her personality was vivacious. The life and soul of the party, she was a flirt, and loved being the centre of attention.

I don't quite know when my feelings for her changed, but they did. I used to drop her home from work occasionally, and when I pulled up outside her flat, she would peck me on the cheek, and say something like: 'I'd love to invite you in for a cup of coffee . . .' Then she'd look me in the eye. 'But you're a married man, and you need to go home to Jacqui.'

'Yeah, OK love, I'll be seeing you,' I'd reply. I would drive away pondering the situation between us. I mean, here she was, a young woman in the prime of her life. Would she really be interested in an old married man like me? Yet, the signals that Donna seemed to be sending out were 'Come and get me! I'm yours for the taking'. Were these thoughts a product of my imagination? Was the cocaine clogging my brain? Or was I just going mad? Whenever we were together, the atmosphere was charged with electricity; it was stimulating me, and I knew it was affecting Donna too. Or was it?

3

COUNTRY CLUB AFFAIR

'The British Heavyweight Champion for 1988 – Arthur White.'

I had done it again. The accolade of the crowds, the hero-worshipping cries, boosted my drug-induced egotistic state of mind. I was flying.

Mingling with the local crowd in Tottenham, I felt like Caesar. My friends and family were there, and their smiles and claps on the back caused my head and heart to swell.

'I'm so proud of you, love!' Jacqui hugged me. She was always there for me, and it made me feel so good, knowing that she was pleased with me.

The months of training had paid off. As well as the steroid-taking, the coke helped to put me in the right frame of mind. It also enhanced the effect of the steroids. I felt marvellous. The European Championships were a couple of months after the British Championships, and they were being held in Germany. Again, I was more than confident that I was going to do well. The pressure was on, because I was competing against the World Champion, Ulf Morrin. He was a tough cookie, but I felt that it was something I could handle. I did it.

'The European Heavyweight Champion for 1988, from Great Britain – Arthur White.'

The national anthem was being blasted out as I stepped off the rostrum. The trophy was a huge affair, which I held above my head, to the cheers of the spectators. Friends of mine who had travelled all the way from England were ecstatic.

The European organizers knew how to put on a 'do'. There was a banquet with an abundance of food and drink, and a live band playing. It was a fantastic end to a fantastic day. I phoned home and told everyone that I had won, and that a grand slam was on the cards. British, European, and the next for me would be the World Title.

Travelling back to our hotel, high in the mountains on the German–Austrian border, the weather suddenly changed. The light of the early evening was instantly swallowed up by a thick darkness. Looking out of the minibus' window, I saw the clouds turn black. Then it started to thunder, with lightning flashing all around. I was frightened, but I didn't show it. My heart thudded and I felt that something was wrong. But what?

At home, I settled back into normal life. I revelled in my new title, and people flocked to me wherever I was. Newspapers reported my win, and I even did a few television interviews. This was the life for me! I started to imagine what response I would get when I brought home the World Title trophy. Snorting coke helped keep my mind buzzing along those lines.

Then, I received a letter.

. . . you have been tested positive at the European Championships. A banned substance was found in both of your urine samples. Therefore, your title has been stripped, and you have now been banned from competing for three years.

I was gutted. I was planning to contest their action, but the truth of the matter was, I was guilty. It would have been useless trying to proclaim my innocence when they had me over a barrel. All I could do was shrug my shoulders and carry on. I decided to join another organization that weren't so stringent in their testing. They opened their arms and welcomed me into their company. They soon shipped me off to South Africa for their World Championships.

I was happy. The weather was great; the people were hospitable; the food was marvellous; and I won. I was competing against a 24-year-old, Thor Kristy. He was shocked that I had beaten him. He was a great bear of a man, and it stunned him that a 38-year-old had knocked him back to second place. This was my first World Title.

The thirteen-and-a-half-hour flight from South Africa went by in a hazy blur. The booze was free so, with two new friends I'd met, both professional golfers, we took advantage of the drinks trolley.

Walking through Heathrow airport I couldn't wait to see Jacqui. As soon as I did, my heart started to beat faster. Half running and half walking, I made my way to her. Throwing our arms around each other, we hugged and kissed.

'Well done, Arthur!' she said.

'Thanks, darling. It's good to be back.'

Jacqui drove us home. Pulling up outside, I was amazed by the decorations that covered the house:

WELL DONE, ARTHUR – WORLD CHAMPION

The whole family had gathered to congratulate me. I was well chuffed! This had made winning the World Title all the more important for me. To be around my family was the best prize that I could have.

Once again, after such a momentous event, I bumped back down to earth. Normality took over as I went to work, and continued to do the things that were a part of my everyday life.

The following week I returned to work at the Country Club. There was a lot of back-slapping, and words of congratulation. There was champagne and cocaine in abundance. I felt great. Life was like a party.

I gave Donna a lift home that night. She was full of praise for me and my achievements. We had a good chat as I drove the car. Then she dropped her bombshell.

'Um . . . I've got somethin' to tell you.'

'What's that, love?'

She took a deep breath. 'I've not been feeling too well recently, so I've decided to go back home to my mum's in Wales.'

Her words took me completely by surprise.

'OK then, love, keep in touch.'

Donna climbed out of the car. 'Bye.'

She didn't offer me her phone number, and I didn't ask. I felt a bit crestfallen as I drove home. But I was quite relieved that she was going away; the temptation to get involved with her was very strong, and I'd escaped that. Yet, on the other hand, I knew I would have liked to have got to know her better.

Within a few weeks, Donna was gone. I left the Country Club soon after, and started to work at another nightclub, Charlie Chan's, in Walthamstow. It was a much better club for me to be working at. Some of the other doormen were my training partners. The money was way better than I was getting at the Country Club, and the clientele were a bit older and better behaved which, all in all, made my working life easier.

One of the barmaids at Chan's was a friend of Donna's. One day, she came up to me and slipped a piece of paper into my hand.

'Donna said to give her a call,' she whispered. As she walked off, I looked at the paper; it had a telephone number on it. I called her a few days later.

During the next few weeks I phoned Donna and we had some really good conversations. Then I was asked to be an official referee at a weightlifting competition in Cardiff, where Donna was living.

When I told her, we made a date to meet up. I was excited! I couldn't wait for the competition to finish so that I could meet up with Donna. I had reserved a table for that evening in the hotel where I was staying.

Standing in the shower, I pondered what the outcome of the evening might be. Never in my married life, up until this point, had I looked at another woman. Jacqui fulfilled me in every way, and therefore there was no need for me to let my mind wander into such fanciful territory. But I have to say that since I had begun door work, the whole world of nightclubbing, drugs, sex and immoral behaviour had become more and more appealing to me. From an early age, I had known who I wanted to marry, and I did. The lifestyle that I was now experiencing was like watching television. I wanted a slice of the action.

The water washed away the soapsuds as I nervously tried to reason with myself. I was a married man, and Donna was just a friend. I wasn't like other men, and I had vowed to be faithful to my wife. And yet . . .

The phone rang. Wrapping a towel around me, I answered it. I replaced the receiver, my heart racing as I tried to get dressed hurriedly. Donna had arrived early, and was on her way up to my room. Buttoning my shirt quickly, I walked over to the door in response to the knocking.

Donna looked radiant. My tongue cleaved to the roof of my mouth and I found it hard to talk to her. But she didn't appear to have any problem being in my company.

'I've booked a table for us,' I mumbled.

She looked me in the eye. 'Un-book it. Let's just sit and talk.'

I did as she said. Then I ordered room service and a couple of bottles of wine.

Needless to say, one thing led to another. Next morning, I had mixed feelings – guilt mingled with excitement. This was the first time that I had spent the night with any woman other than my wife; and a woman who was a great deal younger than me. Cardiff and London were cities full of young, virile men. Yet Donna had chosen *me*.

I had now begun a new 'other' life. Lying and deception became an integral part of it, and my coke habit increased. Donna was still living in Wales and I would phone her often during the week. In order to see her, I had to lay elaborate plans, and cover a lot of mileage. Cardiff was not just around the corner from Essex; yet, my desperation to see her drove me to Wales every Friday.

I had to increase my workload to keep up with the expense of seeing Donna, but eventually, she decided to come back to London. I arranged a flat for her to live in, and a car. To make me look even better in Donna's eyes, I gave her money each week and paid all her debts off. I seemed to be the best thing that had happened to her. She told me about the men she had had relationships with in the past, and how most of them had treated her terribly – I was something different altogether.

My feelings of guilt towards Jacqui diminished as my affair with Donna went on. Jacqui was completely in the dark about it all. Never did I withhold anything such as money from my wife or the children. The only thing they didn't get much of was me. I spun Jacqui lies about needing to work longer hours, and about attending bogus competitions. She swallowed it all.

I was only able to see Donna in between my busy work and home life and it just wasn't enough, for both of us, so we made a plan. Donna had decided that the only way we would be able to be together forever would be if we ran off. I agreed. We both came up with the same destination – South Africa. You couldn't get any further away, as far as we were concerned. I was confident that Jacqui wouldn't discover anything; I was careful not to be seen with Donna in public – we would only meet in the flat.

Everything was heading in the right direction. Soon we would be sitting under the hot sun in South Africa . . . I had already worked out that on the day we left, I would write a note for Jacqui, telling her I was off. But I hit a problem. To enter South Africa you need to obtain a visa. I had the application forms in my briefcase. And Jackie found them.

'What are these?'

'Eh?'

Jacqui held up the forms. She'd been looking in my briefcase for our chequebook.

I made up an excuse and eventually, after many tears and arguments, she believed me. I think tearing up the applications in front of Jacqui reassured her. I hugged and kissed her, knowing that this would comfort her. But I was still trying to figure out how I could get away – I later discovered that I could apply for a visa when I got to South Africa.

My mind was definitely made up; I was leaving my wife and children. My heart had hardened to steel: there was nothing that could change my mind. I had engineered a plan to sell our house. I wanted Jacqui in a smaller place so that when I left, she would be able to keep up the expense of running it. We quickly sold our home, and the guy who bought it paid us a large amount in cash, which I banked.

A week before we moved into the new house, I took off. I left Jacqui a 'Dear John' letter with £500, withdrew £35,000 from our account and set off for a new life in South Africa. I hadn't told a soul that I was going, so when Jacqui tried to find out where I was, she hit a blank wall.

At first, South Africa was everything we expected it to be. We had money to burn. Our days were spent on the beach, and we danced and drank the nights away. Donna used drugs as well, so we would drop lines of coke day in and day out.

Then, when we were at a house party, I met up with a woman who was an expatriate. For some unknown reason, I told her all about my situation.

'It sounds to me like you don't know what, or who, you want,' she remarked.

Until that point, I hadn't thought too much about my wife and children, but that woman's words made me think.

I went to look for Donna, but I couldn't find her. She had left the party, so I searched the streets for her. I found her eventually – she was upset. I hadn't realized it, but she had heard what the woman had said to me.

'You haven't got over Jacqui, have you?'

'I have, but I miss the kids,' I admitted. There was still a part of me that really wanted my wife, but I couldn't say that to Donna.

I couldn't settle after that. Restlessness overtook me. Each day that passed was one of torment. I wasn't interested in the sun and sand any more, and Donna no longer held the same deep attraction for me. I couldn't envisage spending the rest of my life with her. But, and it was the 'but' that caused my mind to spin like a revolving door, there wasn't anyone that I could confide in. Slowly, my life was becoming like a hell in paradise.

I knew there was only one course of action open to me. I had to go home.

Donna was quiet as I packed the holdall full of my necessities: namely, drugs.

'I'll be back,' I said.

At London airport, Jacqui didn't seem to recognize me. I had lost weight, I looked drawn, and was unshaven. For the last few weeks, sleep had eluded me. I had tried to blot out my troubled thoughts with alcohol, but that hadn't worked. I was in a state. Jacqui, being the wonderful woman that she is, welcomed me into her arms. It was as if I had just returned from one of my many weightlifting trips abroad. We stood like that, locked in each other's arms for a while, as the bustle of the airport swirled around us.

'Come on, Arthur, let me take you home.'

I handed her my holdall: 'Get rid of that, Jacq. What's in there has been the cause of all my troubles.'

Christmas was around the corner. I had chosen the right time to be at home, and even my children had forgiven me. I promised Jacqui, with my hand on my heart, that I would never leave her – *never*. Jacqui's eyes spoke volumes to me. I could see that she really wanted to trust and believe me, but she just wasn't sure.

Within a couple of days, I had broken my promise. New Year's Eve 1989 saw me pack my bags and leave my wife – again. I had phoned Donna's mum in Wales. She had told me that Donna was due back home soon, and I decided that I would meet her. What I had done to Donna was very wrong – leaving her in South Africa alone was an awful thing to have done. I worked out in my confused mind that I should do the right thing and make it up to her.

The day I left for Wales was torture. I walked along the road towards the train station, with my holdall. Jacqui and the children were driving along at a snail's pace in the car, as they tearfully pleaded with me to stay with them. The scene tore at my heartstrings. But not enough to convince me that staying would be good for them, or me.

My reunion with Donna was, at first, full of recriminations. But after a couple of drinks and a meal she soon came round to my way of thinking. Throughout the time I spent with Donna, I felt that I wanted to spend the rest of my life with her and she believed me. Donna didn't want to live in Wales, and I didn't, so I managed to rent a flat in Sawbridgeworth, and began another 'new life' with Donna.

But life is a funny thing. Sometimes you can have everything that your heart desires, and yet you're still not happy. Donna, who seemed perfect to me in every way, didn't do that much for me when we lived together. So, once again, I did my disappearing act. I left her.

4

DEBT COLLECTOR

'There he goes. Watch that man. He's evil.'

'He's working for Joe. Keep clear of 'im.'

'The guy's tooled up. He nearly killed Jimmy.'

I could hear the voices of the men as I strolled through Spitalfields fruit and vegetable market in Bishopsgate, London. My trench coat flapped open as I looked from side to side at the different wholesale stands. I wanted to laugh. One fight, and now I was reputed to be as bad as one of the Krays.

The fight had taken place the night before, in The Gun pub, in Bishopsgate. My brother's friend, Joe, was a rich man, who owned a wholesale business in the market. His turnover was millions of pounds each year. He was having a problem with the market traders. He operated a credit system whereby you bought the goods, sold them, and then you paid what you owed. Unfortunately, some of the men were unscrupulous, and had no intention of paying Joe the money that they owed him. Jimmy fell into that category.

That evening, Joe was boozing whilst I was drinking Pepsi. I had taken some lines of coke to keep me alert. Joe got into an argument with Jimmy, and Jimmy whacked him on the chin. Joe fell on the table, and landed on the floor. He was not a fighter, and I knew that if he didn't get any help, he'd be in serious trouble. So I stepped in. Grabbing hold of Jimmy, I smacked him in the mouth. A full bottle of champagne was on the bar; I hit Jimmy across the face with it. As he staggered back, I hit him again. Jimmy didn't know what was happening to him, but I wasn't finished yet. I was well aware that I had to prove myself to Joe. The whole point of meeting him that evening had been to make an agreement about being his debt collector.

My speciality was to 'throat' somebody. Being a champion dead-lifter, my grip was like a vice: I would grab someone by the throat, which would quickly cut off their air supply, causing them to faint. Their arms would go limp, and just before they passed out, I would give them one powerful smack, which sorted them out. Jimmy experienced my technique.

I dragged him through the bar doors, and continued to beat him. By now, he certainly wasn't able to put up any resistance. I took his keys out of his pockets, opened up the door of his Mercedes, and threw him onto the front seats. Blood was pouring out of him like a leaky kettle. I told him in no uncertain terms that if he didn't pay Joe what he owed him, he would be getting more of the same, but in double doses. He paid.

Joe was ecstatic about my performance. He was confident that he would recover all that was owed to him, and he had his own personal bodyguard – me. Because Joe was pleased with me, he paid me £5,000 as a retainer. This money was a sort of down payment on any future work I carried out on Joe's behalf. I felt good that once again I had some decent cash.

Now, it was after 2 a.m., and as I walked through Spitalfields, the tale of my exploits had already reached the market traders. Although the situation seemed comical to me, I knew that some of the punters that I would have to deal with wouldn't be such easy pushovers as Jimmy. The nature of the job meant I needed to kit myself out. I needed to get tooled up.

That very afternoon, I found a shop in Leyton near to where I was now renting a bedsit – it sold fishing accessories. I purchased a twelve-inch diver's knife. The shiny steel blade made me feel well able to deal with any punter that dared to challenge me. The knife case had two straps which, normally, divers would wear strapped to the outside of their leg. I fastened it to the inside of my forearm, with the handle pointing down to my wrist. It made access to the knife easier in an emergency. Then I got a list of names from Joe of the people that owed him money. My days were spent visiting various markets, collecting Joe's dosh.

I met up with one guy called Ted in the Camden Lock market. He was very reluctant to pay up, and didn't like being threatened by the likes of me.

'Listen, mate.' He pointed his finger in my face. 'I know Lenny McClean. He'll sort you out.'

I knew of Lenny. I shrugged my shoulders. 'I'll see about that. I'll be back.'

Lenny McClean was known in the East End of London as The Guv'nor. He was a prizefighter who could never be beaten. People were terrified of him, and you never used his name lightly unless you were sure he was on your side. I had met up with Lenny some years previously when we were training together in a gym. I knew of his fighting skills, and he knew of my strength in powerlifting. We showed each other a fair bit of respect. I never doubted for one moment that he feared me, but I knew that I couldn't cross him. So I used my 'loaf'.

Lenny was working at the Hippodrome nightclub in Leicester Square, London. I went to the club to meet him. The bouncers on the door didn't want to let me into the club initially.

'Who are you?' they asked.

'I've come to see Lenny. Tell him Arthur White wants to see him.'

Two of them walked off. Within minutes they returned.

'Follow us.'

They led me to a dark little office at the end of a corridor. Lenny was as large as life, all 19½ stone of him, dressed in a dog's-tooth check jacket. His voice was gruff as he greeted me.

''Ello, son!'

I told him about Ted, the guy from Camden Lock market, threatening me with Lenny's name, and filled him in on Joe's story, and the money he was owed. He agreed to come and work with me – it was an easy way for him to earn a few quid.

Turning to leave, Lenny said: 'That'll cost you a monkey (£500).'

I paid him then and there. Lenny was now on my firm, which meant I had a lot of power.

My reputation grew in leaps and bounds. Many people thought I was Lenny's younger brother: we looked quite alike. I never dispelled those rumours; it was good for business. We were very successful in our debt collecting. When we turned up, people got scared, which meant they coughed up the dough quickly. It was a lucrative business. Whatever we amassed for the day's work, we creamed off our percentage first, and gave Joe the rest.

The following week, I went back to see Ted from the Camden Lock market. I mentioned Lenny was now on my firm. He paid up straight away.

There was one guy called Johnny. He owed Joe a small fortune. Johnny was like a shadow – very elusive – he was hard to track down. I discovered where his office was and one day I broke into it, and smashed it up. I left a message with the guy in the office next to him: 'Tell Johnny that I'll be back.'

Early one morning, at Spitalfields, Johnny came to Joe's stand. He didn't see me at first, and I never gave him a chance to react. I pounced on him like a cat after a mouse. I 'throated' him, and threw him against a palette-load of tomatoes – 144 boxes. He and the tomatoes went flying. I kicked the squashed boxes of tomatoes out of my path to get a strong grip on Johnny again, and really sorted him out. Being a shrewd man, he settled a large part of his debt and skulked off, licking his wounds. But he knew that my debt collecting was illegal and he turned up a few hours later with the police, who cautioned me. Johnny obviously thought that once he had got the police onto me, I would back off. He didn't know me. I found out where he lived and then threatened to burn his garage down . . . along with his house. I was determined to win. I guess Johnny knew I was getting too close for comfort and, eventually, he coughed up. It was a nice little earner for me.

Most of the time people paid, but there were always one or two of them who thought they were a bit clever and could give me a knock-back. Billy was one of them. He was a wide boy who thought he was razor-sharp. He owned a number of fruit stalls, but he was forever dodging Joe. He didn't want to pay up.

'Fancy a drive in the country, Lenny?' I asked one day.

'All right, boy.'

We motored to Epping, where Billy had a large stall in the street market. We walked up to him.

'It's pay-up time.'

'But I 'aven't got it!'

'You've owed ten grand for a long time. I want the first instalment.'

'Look, see me next week and . . .'

'No, *you* look. I want two grand *now*. We'll talk about the rest later.'

While I was busy negotiating terms and conditions, Lenny, who was standing beside me, was getting agitated. He had a lot of nervous energy building up. He suddenly let out a bestial roar and, hooking his hands under the corner of the stall, he turned the lot over. The contents flew through the air, spewing into the road and over the pavement. Women started screaming. Traffic was halted because oranges and apples, cabbages and potatoes were flying everywhere. Not wanting to be outdone by Lenny, I grabbed Billy by the throat and his leather belt, and turned him upside down. The contents of his pockets fell on the floor, and his money pouch emptied all over the ground.

'Put me down!'

I threw him on the ground.

'Don't hurt me – don't hurt me!' We weren't mucking about, and he knew it. He gathered up the money which was scattered all over the street. I took it.

'I'll be back next week, Billy,' I said, calmly. 'So be ready.'

As we drove away, I glanced in the rear-view mirror at the mess we'd left behind. I grinned at Lenny.

'A good morning's work. 'Ere's your monkey, mate.'

◆　　◆　　◆

The orange-flavoured 'Jubbly' produced the desired effect. I thought that the triangular ice-pop would do the trick in numbing my neck, making it easier to cut – thus ending my life. I had bought it that morning at about 5 o'clock from the corner shop. When I'd asked for it, the shopkeeper had looked at me as though I was crazy. I suppose it was a strange thing for someone to request in December.

Driving through Homerton, east London, I knew it was the right time. I turned into a side road. The morning was dark and cold, reflecting how I was feeling inside. Tears ran down my face. For the last few days I hadn't slept and whenever my eyes became tired, I would lay on my bed with a towel over them. My cocaine consumption had increased to a new high. All the money that I was earning was being snorted up my nose. I didn't care. Cocaine was my only companion. The bedsit I was renting was bereft of life and warmth. I had to push all thoughts of being at home with my wife and kids completely out of my mind. Even Donna wasn't that interested in me now. She was after someone else.

Living no longer held any pleasure. Death was beckoning with powerful arms, waiting to engulf me. The familiar shroud of blackness slowly, stealthily, crept over me. I welcomed it. Leaning my head back against the headrest, I tried to gain control of the battle that was raging inside. My heart was crying out for help – help from someone, *anyone*, to stop me from doing what I had set out to do to myself; help from someone to sort my life out; help from someone to just *help* me. Yet my mind was closing the lid on my life: 'It's too late. There's *no one*. You're all alone, mate. That's it. Finito. Finished. Done. Dead.'

Sobs broke out from my lips. 'Oh, Jacqui, what have I done?'

My mind jumped from the faces of my father, my mother, my siblings, my children, from people that I knew, to the people that I had given a hard time to. No one was here for me now. The 'Jubbly' had numbed my neck. I withdrew the diver's knife from its sheath.

The dawn was breaking – it was now or never. Lifting the blade up, I looked at myself in the rear-view mirror. Those eyes that reflected back weren't mine. The blackness in them seemed to have no end. Shutting them tight, I gripped the handle of the knife and placed the blade against my cheek.

Time stood still.

For what seemed like an eternity, the blade slowly opened up the skin of my cheek, sliced through my neck, and down across my chest. Blood spurted out like a garden hose. With my eyes still shut, I sensed the warm stickiness of my blood, pumping out all over me. I wondered how long it would take for my heart to realize that my blood was no longer coursing around my body. I managed to replace the knife in its sheath. A heaviness weighed me down. This is it, I thought. My last few moments on earth. Fleetingly, I wondered where I was going; I hoped that it would bring the relief from this life that I desperately needed.

Dying was taking a bit of a time.

I started the car and drove deeper into the East End of London. My hope was that I would lose consciousness, and crash the car. That would definitely be the end of me. I briefly thought about the other people who would be involved in the accident . . . but the truth was, I didn't care. I just wanted out of this miserable existence.

Unfortunately, the blood that half an hour ago was being pumped out had now dwindled to a halt. My clotting agents were working overtime. The realization that I was going to live caused me to break down in a torrent of tears and anguish. Could I do nothing right?

Turning the car around, I headed back to my bleak bedsit. Stripping off my bloodied clothes, I felt only despair.

From then on, everything became an effort. Somehow I forced myself to go to work. I didn't see any point in hanging around my bedsit. Maybe I could earn enough to buy a big stash of gear, and blow my brains out. Walking through Spitalfields, I noticed that people were looking at me on the sly. Nobody questioned me about the cut on my face and I let them reach their own conclusions. They probably assumed that I had been in a violent fight. They would have been right. The fight had been with myself.

♦   ♦   ♦

The hot Tenerife sun beat down on my skin with a vengeance. I was tanked up with coke and cheap wine.

I was with Donna. We'd decided to hop on a plane and see some of the world. The fact that for nearly two weeks we had hardly communicated with each other didn't disturb me too much. We had gone through the motions of trying to resurrect our relationship, but I knew, really, it was dead. Still, I tried to enjoy myself, regardless. My mood, even on holiday, was a yo-yo of confusion. One minute I would be flying high, the next, I would plunge into the depths of depression.

Early one morning, I took myself off to the beach, alone. I had just called Jacqui at home, and told her a pack of lies.

'I'm here on business, love.'

'On business – in Tenerife? Don't take me for a fool, Arthur.'

'No, no, straight up, Jacqui! I'm collecting money.'

Replacing the handset, I knew she didn't believe me. Why had I rung her? Just a weird compulsion to hear her voice . . . Now, she was even more suspicious of me. I shouldn't have bothered.

Sitting on the beach, I watched the sun grow brighter and brighter as the day broke forth in all its brilliance. It was difficult for me to think clearly. This was paradise – but I was in sheer hell and torment. The waves were gently lapping to and fro. What should have put me in a tranquil mood stirred up giant feelings of guilt, remorse, anger, sadness and loneliness. The motion of the waves was enticing. It was so tempting to just stand up and stride towards their beckoning call. Taking deep breaths, I was just about to walk off into a watery grave, when a voice said: *'You cannot take your own life.'*

There was no one around. I looked up into the cloud-less sky.

'Who are you?'

Anyone going by would have assumed that I was a regular fruitcake if they'd heard me talking to myself.

Then the voice answered: *'I am your Father.'*

Snorting, I replied, 'You're not my dad. My dad's dead.'

I waited for an answer. I thought I had glimpsed a face among the clouds, but I couldn't be sure. Shaking my head, I suddenly realized that I had finally flipped my lid.

'I'm going crazy,' I muttered.

I forgot about topping myself. Instead, I went back to the hotel and did a few lines of coke to block everything out.

The holiday was soon over. Walking through customs at Stansted airport, Donna and I probably looked like all the other sun-baked, relaxed holidaymakers, but in reality that was far from the truth.

Relatives and friends were in the arrivals hall, waiting to meet their loved ones. I didn't notice that Jacqui was among them.

I called her later to tell her that I was home. I was sticking to my story about being on a business trip. And then she said, 'I saw you both.'

Those words were like a sharp knife piercing me, right down to the bone. I would have continued to lie, but Jacqui had caught me out. I slammed down the phone.

After a couple of weeks in the sun, nothing had been resolved. Increasingly, death looked like the way out. It was either that, or killing someone else and losing my liberty.

5

FRESH START

I was bent over my victim, pinning him to the tarmac with my knee. My left hand was wrapped around his head, as he lay immobilized on his left side. In my right hand I held my knife. Murder was not on my mind, but teaching him a lesson was. I began to saw behind his ear lobe. My intention was to cut off his ear.

And then I heard a voice.

'Arthur! Stop!'

♦   ♦   ♦

How had it come to this? The guy was a stranger to me. He was at my mercy because of Donna. I barely saw her now; even our telephone conversations were a thing of the past. I was missing her, but only because I was lonely. I missed my wife, too, but that was a different thing altogether. I *really* missed Jacqui. It was painful to say her name, let alone think about her; that would have been torture.

The bedsit at Leyton was never truly home to me. It was somewhere for me to rest my aching body, wash, and change my clothing. One night I was having forty winks, when the buzzer for the front door sounded.

'It's me, Donna. I need to see you.'

Something was very wrong. I could tell by the tone of her voice. She was in tears as she told me her problem. The 'problem' was a man, and it was drug-related. Donna's main concern was that in the altercation she'd had with the guy, she had come off worse, and she couldn't live with that.

'Please could you sort him out?' she begged me. 'No way do I want him to get away with it. He needs to be taught a lesson!'

I was dressed in my jogging bottoms, with a singlet. The diver's knife was strapped to my arm, as usual, for all the world to see. The cold February night air chilled my exposed skin. I made my way to my car. Donna was up ahead, leading the way back to the nightclub in north London where her troubles had started. I parked my car in Tottenham High Road and we walked round the corner to the club. It was now about 1 a.m. The doors opened; people were spilling out onto the street.

In full view of the club punters, I stood with legs apart, arms by my sides, fists balled, ready for action. Rambo had nothing on me. Donna was standing just behind me. A man appeared at the door amidst a crowd of people.

'That's him, Arthur!'

The guy who'd had the run-in with Donna must have recognized her then, because he broke free from his mates, and legged it. I was in hot pursuit. I hadn't taken any gear recently, but it was still in my system from the last hit. This guy was not going to get away. Adrenaline was pulsing through my body. For that moment in time, its effect was better than cocaine. I was buzzing.

The club was situated at the top of a dead-end street. At the far end was a wall. The guy that I was pursuing hadn't done himself any favours by running down that street. There was no escape – he was trapped. He ran around a parked van. I grabbed the roof rack with one hand, and vaulted over the top of the van, landing in front of him. The guy turned to flee, so I stabbed him once in the back. He continued to run, so I stabbed him again. He stumbled and fell, and I pounced on him like a tiger. In shock, the guy feebly tried to resist me, but I was in my element now. To keep him still I gave him a couple of punches to his body and his head. That stopped him. His right ear stood out to me, like a flashing neon light. That's when the idea of cutting it off came to me. And I would have completed the job, had it not been for the body-less voice.

'Arthur! Stop!'

Glancing around, I could see that no one was there. Yet I had clearly, audibly, heard someone call my name. The voice had broken my concentration. I put my knife back into its sheath, and stood up.

As I turned round, I was shocked to the core. In front of me was a crowd of about two hundred people. Whilst I had been busy doing a butcher's job on the guy, the night revellers had congregated in a mass behind me. I knew that somewhere among the crowd would be my victim's mates. I guessed I was in for a hiding. Being kicked about is no fun and I was worried that someone might have a knife.

I began to walk slowly towards them, preparing myself for a fight. No way was I going down begging for mercy. Strength seemed to come from the air as I continued to walk forward. I tried to catch people's eyes as the distance between us shortened. But as I reached the edge of the mob, and just as I was bracing myself for the first blow, something strange happened. The crowd parted and formed two sides, with a path down the middle. I hesitated. Was this a trick? Would I get half way, only for them to close ranks – and that's the last of me? No. I walked through the crowd to safety.

I got to my car. Revving the engine, it suddenly dawned on me that Donna had disappeared. I didn't worry about that for long. What was the point? Within a short time, I was home, dressed and off to work. I put the whole incident out of my mind.

◆   ◆   ◆

By now, my drug habit was costing me hugely. As soon as I earned a few quid, it would slip through my fingers, and down my throat, or up my nose. The bedsit was proving too expensive, so I decided to give it up. But where could I go? At that point, I had left my wife and the children six times. Jacqui wasn't keen to take me back again and I didn't blame her! The level of trust between Donna and me was zero, so being with her wasn't an option either. There was only one place I knew I'd be welcome.

'No problem, son. Any time!'

'Thanks, Mum.'

I wondered what my mother would think if she found out what I was up to. Mum was from a different era, and the drug culture was far removed from her way of life. The depressive, suicidal mood that I had drifted into was permanently a part of my sad life. There just didn't seem any point to anything. I took as much cocaine as I could get into my body. But I began to notice it wasn't having the same mind-blowing effects that it used to, so I took more and more to achieve that high.

About 4 o'clock one morning, after leaving work, I had snorted some coke to pep myself up for some debt collecting. I was working alone now, which wasn't bad; still, if I needed to call on Lenny, I could. Cruising along

Eastway in Leyton, a car behind me tooted and flashed. Initially, I ignored the driver, but he did it a second time. Anger sprang up like a volcano erupting. I pulled over to let him overtake me. Then, I gunned the engine and tore after him. He began to drive more quickly. I flashed and tooted him. He kept looking at me in his rear-view mirror. I could sense his fear; I just wanted to pulverize him. He drove into a cul-de-sac, and without parking or turning the engine off, leapt out of his car and took off, disappearing into a block of flats. I walked up to his car and turned the engine off. Taking his car keys, I flung them down the nearest drain.

I scanned the dark flats for any sign of life. Nothing.

'C'mon, show yer face! C'mon! Let's see how brave you are now!' I yelled at the top of my voice.

No response.

My anger spilled into the night air as I filled the emptiness with expletives. I had psyched myself up for a good fight. Now, I could only plug the hole with more drugs.

◆　◆　◆

I was trying to make amends with Jacqui. We were on speaking terms, and I kept hoping she might forgive me, but I didn't want to push her too far too soon. So I was keeping my feelings hidden for now. I had come to terms with the fact that my relationship with Donna was, in reality, history. I would romanticize to myself that this younger woman was interested in me – but in truth, I didn't want her any more. I knew that in an ideal world, Jacqui and I and the children would be reconciled and living together as one big happy family. Still, real life had me still sleeping at my mum's. My mother wasn't happy with my situation; I know she was hoping that Jacqui and I would get back together, if only for the sake of the children. My mum had old-fashioned views about family life.

But all of my 'nice family' dreams were wrecked one Saturday morning in February. Donna would periodically call me at my mum's, just for a chat. Unfortunately, Jacqui had chosen that morning to pop in and see me, and she overheard my conversation with Donna. It wasn't the content that troubled her; it was the fact that Donna and I were still in contact with each other. As soon as I put the phone down, Jacqui erupted. It wasn't long before we were shouting and screaming at each other. The air was thick with my lies and deception.

'That's it! Never again. We are *finished*.' Jacqui stormed out of the front door without a backward glance. It was then that it really hit me that I was alone; I'd been acting so selfishly towards her, only really thinking about myself. I knew then, in my heart of hearts, that this was the end of the long and turbulent road with my wife.

I felt adrift from the rest of the human race. That night I went out and got hammered. I consumed so much coke and alcohol that it was amazing that I remained standing. From that point on, I went on a bender. I would try to consume as much as I could. I really wanted to kill myself but the next best thing, as far as I was concerned, was to be so out of it that I was only half-aware of the real world.

I decided to meet up with a friend one night, on the other side of the River Thames. We drank ourselves under the table, and afterwards I set off, in a terrible state, for home. Blackheath was a fair distance from where my mum lived. Driving along the lonely road, I noticed a sign for Crystal Palace – I was going the wrong way. I spun the car around and headed back the way I had come. I have no idea what happened after that – I had a complete blackout.

A cold breeze ruffled my thin silk shirt. Stirring from my 'bed', I sat up. Even in my muddled state of mind, I could see that I had fallen asleep out in the open. To be more precise, I had taken refuge on a bench on Tower Bridge. The water swished beneath me. The early birds were flying up above me. How did I get there? Dazed I looked around. Where was my car? My tongue was like sandpaper, and my head was spinning. Staggering to my feet, I wasn't sure where I should go. My feet seemed to know, so I followed them.

I ended up on Westminster Bridge. The thirty-minute walk woke me up. My car was parked on the bridge, with the keys still in the ignition. I climbed in and drove home.

I was seriously worried. Up until now, I had been able to handle whatever had happened to me. Having blackouts was another thing altogether. Where had that time gone? I realized that I needed help, and I needed it now.

◆　　◆　　◆

In 1990, when she was 13, Emma had joined a youth group at Epping Forest Community Church. She had been invited by a school friend. As the months went by, Emma became a Christian, and later that year was baptized. She encouraged my wife and my son that it would be the best thing for them too! Neither Jacqui nor I had ever had the inclination to go to church. It had never dawned on us that we should go, or even send our children. Christian living was not something that we had thought about – although if anyone had asked whether we were Christians or not, the answer would have been 'yes'. At least, before I went off the rails. We, along with

many others, thought that being born in England, a
so-called 'Christian' country, automatically gave us the
right to label ourselves 'Christian'! I didn't know much
about this Christian business. In fact, I didn't *want* to
know. Christianity was for wimps, I thought. What good
was it for a 17-stone heavyweight World Champion
powerlifter?

A man called Vincent Wiffin was an elder of the
church that my daughter Emma attended. Jacqui had
recommended him to me. It was Jacqui who told me
what I already knew – that I was in desperate need of
professional help. I felt I had no option but to contact
this Vincent guy.

When I first met Vin in 1993, I was a bit taken aback.
Here, clearly, was no wimp. I was expecting him to be a
bearded, long-haired, pebbly-spectacled, sandal-wear-
ing freak. But Vin wasn't like that. He was no fool. He
was a big guy, and could clearly handle himself. I had
strapped my knife to my leg, as I usually did. I didn't
figure he would be too much trouble for me, but I was-
n't taking any chances. He knew more about me than I
did about him, and that was a disadvantage in my book,
but I kept cool and listened to what he had to say.

Meeting up with Vincent changed my life. It sounds a
bit of a cliché, but for me it is absolutely true. Quickly,
we built up a rapport. He didn't preach to me, or bash
me over the head with his Bible, or shout 'Sinner, sinner,
get thee hence!' which I was half-expecting. It would
have given me a good excuse to get up and walk out.

Relating my life up until that point to Vin helped me
to put my thoughts into perspective. I think it opened up
a whole new world for him, too! I was a first for Vin. He
later confessed that he had never met anyone quite like
me before, and had been somewhat apprehensive about
meeting me. His background was very different from

mine. Living in a sleepy, middle-class village in Essex, he had not been exposed to the likes of me, and my lifestyle.

Standing on his doorstep saying our goodbyes, Vin said a few words to me that have remained with me all my life. He said, 'Arthur, you have to choose.'

As I walked away, his words gutted me more than anything else he had said to me at that meeting. I had to choose between Jacqui and Donna? I had to choose between my two beautiful children, or starting another family? Ultimately, I had to choose between good and evil. I had gone from a good life, with my family and job, and peace of mind, to a life full of evil, drugs, violence, and an immoral relationship. At this place in my life, there was no peace of mind *or* heart. As for love – the capacity to love others, to receive their love, and to love myself had gone from me. I was full of contempt for myself. Looking at others, I could see my own problems reflected in people's faces; many people were selfish, and so consumed with themselves that they didn't even realize that love was missing from their lives.

I had thought I had reached rock bottom before, but this time it was different. I felt that I was on the road of no return.

It was a cold March morning when, in Spitalfields market car park, I stood looking up at the sky with my arms outstretched and called out, 'Help me, God!' I didn't know if that was how you should pray, but it was the best I could do, in my desperation. 'God! If you're so clever, you come and sort it out!'

There were no angels' wings flapping, no trumpets blowing, the sky didn't open up and belch forth any weird and wonderful manifestations. Absolutely nothing. And yet a strange feeling enveloped me, soothing me – and I felt at peace with myself.

I wasted no time in making a new start. I unstrapped my precious diver's knife, and threw it into a skip nearby. Back home at my mum's, I took the drastic step of emptying my cache of drugs onto the kitchen table. Mum gasped in horror at the sight, taking in the fact that her darling youngest son was a drug addict.

I felt the need to share with people the new path that I had now chosen for my life. Vin was thrilled, and congratulated me. He took me under his wing, and showed me that following Jesus Christ was the only answer for my life, and that I would never again sink to those depths of depravity, as long as I stuck close by Jesus.

I met with Vin, over the weeks that followed, for marriage guidance counselling, then for Bible study and prayer. As I continued to meet with him, my feelings of self-worth increased. Vin was instrumental in getting Jacqui and I back together again. Although Jacqui wasn't a Christian yet, she was well known in the church, and some of the members were apprehensive about us getting back together too quickly. They were worried that I could be using God as an excuse to get back with Jacqui. She wasn't convinced that I could change so quickly, anyway.

The going was very slow and I missed my family desperately. I had a picture of them beside my bed which I would sometimes hold tightly, sobbing my heart out, wanting so much to be with them. The pain was awful. Jesus had now given me a new ability to love, and because I wasn't able to fully put it to use, it was causing an aching and emptiness. Out of the depth of my heartache for Jacqui and the children, I cried out to God: 'Lord, if it's not your will for us to be together, I'll accept it. But I will never go back to the life I once lived, and turn away from you.'

I knew I had to pray that prayer: I wanted Jesus to know that I was truly his, and his alone, but I still desperately wanted my family back.

A few days later, Jacqui called me. It was 9.30 in the evening.

'Arthur, would you like to come over for a chat?'

As soon as I had put the phone down, I was up the stairs, two at a time. I showered and shaved, and splashed on aftershave in what must have been record time.

We sat and talked until about 3 o'clock in the morning. Jacqui wanted to take things slowly, to see whether there was any truth in what I was telling her. Time would tell!

As I stood at the front door, I asked her if she still loved me.

'I've always loved you, Arthur. It's just that I can't trust you. I need to be sure.'

My hopes shot up. I believed then that God was doing something in my wife. I was hoping that soon we would be together again. However, before my hopes came to fruition, I had to square things with my children. This was a painful time for me. Again, it made me realize that my selfish lifestyle had caused a great deal of hurt to many people. My fear was that my children would reject me. What would I do then?

I sat them down one afternoon and told them about my life for the past seven years.

'Kids, I have got to tell you both that your dad was a drug addict.'

A lump formed in my throat, making it hard for me to speak. As I recounted my sorry excuse for a life, tears flowed like a river, cascading down my face and falling into my lap. My two lovely children, unspoiled by the world, cried along with me. The loss of our beautiful house, and the one in Spain, not to mention the fact that I let about £150,000 slip through my fingers (or, more precisely, snorted up my nose) . . . I had even stooped so low as to sell my wedding ring. At that time of debauched living, nothing had been precious to me. Everything was expendable.

My children were wonderful.

'Dad,' they said, 'we're more proud of you now than of anything you've ever done in the past.'

I couldn't believe that they were so forgiving. The fact that my children had not turned their backs on me encouraged me to think that perhaps Jesus Christ wouldn't either.

6

CONFLICT AND COMMITMENT

Walking through Spitalfields market early in the morning was a trial for me. Men nodded as I passed by, my presence causing a flicker of fear to cross their faces. I knew I looked menacing with my spotless white trench coat collar turned up, smart trousers and polished brown shoes. I was the business. No one messed with me, and that was the way it should be so that I could collect money owed to my boss. Yet deep down I was uneasy. Around the market my nickname was 'The Animal', which did not reflect my new status as a Christian. I was no longer working for Joe. I had got another job, still debt collecting, but it was legitimate and I was on PAYE with a large company in the market. I was happy to work in this way for a while as I was paying my taxes and I knew this was pleasing to God.

The problem for me was how I had to go about collecting the debts. Violence, aggression, invoking threats and fear was becoming more and more difficult to impose. My life was incongruous. It was not balanced and harmonious. I would wake up in the morning and read my Bible. Driving to work, my car was filled with gospel music and I would be praising God because I was so full of joy. Then, I would get to work and switch from being peaceful and at one with the Lord to being a nasty, unpleasant, vicious person. I so much wanted to tell people about my new life. I wanted to tell them that they too needed Jesus. I wanted them to know how dramatically my life had changed since I received Jesus as my Lord and Saviour. There were still times when my ego was boosted when people showed me respect – through fear. It seemed so wrong and I wasn't quite sure what to do. I would struggle, wrestling with my thoughts and how I ought to behave in order to get the money owed. There had to be another way.

One morning I was in Dino's café at about 4 a.m. I had been asking the Lord, 'What can I do to let people know about you?' The café was packed with all the market traders, wholesale and retail, about sixty men. What would happen if I started to talk about Jesus? I was very aware of what people would think of me, and was frightened of other people's perception of me. Would they think I was mad? That I'd gone soft? That I was now a pushover?

Dino suddenly spoke to me. 'Arthur . . . ' He was looking me up and down. 'You look . . . well, you look *different*. In fact, you look like a film star, mate.'

His words made me feel warm inside, and I smiled at him. As I did so, my mouth seemed to open up.

'Well, Dino, that's because I've become a born-again Christian.'

An immediate silence fell upon the whole café. Newspapers didn't rustle, voices were not heard, people didn't move. I had everyone's attention!

'Oh? I'm – well – uh . . . that's . . . good for you.' Dino shoved a bag at me. 'Here's your salt beef sandwich.' And he swiftly moved on to the next customer.

I turned and left. Munching on my sandwiches I knew that I had stepped through an open door that could not be closed. It wouldn't be long before everyone in the market would know that I was a Christian. That thought caused me a bit of anxiety. Still, I wasn't going to worry about it; I was confident that the Lord would see me through.

I was soon put to the test. I had to collect some money from a guy called Stan. He had never given me any problems. But this particular day, as I stood in front of him with my black book open in the palm of my hand and said, 'Stan, you owe this much,' he looked me in the eye, swore, and said, 'I'll pay when I'm ready.' Then he turned his back on me.

I was in a dilemma. This had never happened to me before. Traders usually paid up, or promised that they would soon. My reputation was such that no one dared to defy me – until now. My initial reaction was to grab Stan by the shoulder and wallop him. But I couldn't, not now, not since I had become a Christian.

'Stan! Look, mate. I don't want to argue about this. I want to sort this out peaceful without any problems.'

He turned and looked at me disdainfully.

Now what? I thought.

'I'm a changed man, Stan. I'm a Christian, and I don't want no violence. Here, have this.' I pulled a *Why Jesus* booklet out of my pocket and handed it to him. He took it, and without looking at it, walked off.

This type of response became a pattern for my working life in the market. Some men would pay up when I asked them, but some guys would challenge me and I had to restrain myself. Some people were wary and thought I might go berserk and kill them because 'God told me to do it', which did make me laugh a bit. But I really wanted them to know the truth of the gospel and how it had affected and changed me, and could do the same for them too.

I was in a constant state of mental conflict. When men tried to take me on, I had to make snap decisions about how to handle the situation. I wasn't successful all the time, but I knew that the more I followed Jesus the more I would be able to overcome my natural way of doing things.

Returning to the offices one morning I caught one of the drivers in the act of stealing some of the fruit. He was loading produce from the van into his car.

'Oi!' I shouted. 'What do you think you're doing?'

He swore, and carried on piling stuff into his car. 'What's it got to do with you?'

'What's it got to do with me?' I was seething. '*This* is what it's got to do with me.'

I grabbed him by the scruff of the neck, and hauled him up against the wall, pinning him with my arms so that he couldn't move. Suddenly, all my suppressed anger and frustration from the past months came out and I let this man have it. I swore, I ranted and raved. I shook him and his eyes bulged with fear. Dropping him like a sack of potatoes, I stormed off.

Then the Lord spoke to me. I knew it was Jesus, because what he said wouldn't have come into my mind before I became a Christian.

'What you did to that man was wrong.'

Immediately I knew I had to go back to the guy and apologize. This was very hard for me because I would have a tarnished reputation. Of course, that would mean nothing to God, but it was a dent to my ego! I thought about what would happen. The word would spread like wildfire and the hardcore traders may get it into their heads to take me on. Still, I went back, and like an obedient child told the guy that I was sorry that I'd handled him aggressively. I added that I would have to tell the boss about his pilfering and he would probably lose his job. He wasn't happy, but I was happy! I knew that I would have to think on my feet every day as I encountered these situations. I also knew that I would have to be looking to God daily to help and guide me in how I was to conduct myself in this world.

♦   ♦   ♦

Living at my mum's was a lonely time for me. Although it was comfortable – she couldn't do enough for me; I suppose for her it was like old times, fussing over me, cooking and doing my washing – I could sense she didn't trust me. I think she was a bit scared of me, of what I was capable of doing.

I had bought myself a wooden boat kit, and most evenings I was building the boat in my bedroom – alone. I tried not to think about the drug scene I had left behind. I was purposely keeping a low profile, staying away from certain people and places. I knew if I didn't, I would be dragged back and immersed in filth and degradation. The buzz I would get from cocaine, and the feeling the steroids gave me of being invincible, the party atmosphere that wrapped it all together . . . I did miss it at times, but I had to learn to cut the thought of my past life out of my mind. And of course, the past included Donna. I was well aware that thoughts can give rise to actions, so it was imperative that my mind was under control.

Donna . . . I felt I was really over her. I had no desire to even want to know her again. But then out of the blue, she called and wanted to see me.

'Arthur,' she said, 'I'm pregnant and I don't want the baby. I've got to get rid of it.'

There was no way the child was mine. By now, I hadn't seen or heard from Donna for a long time. She told me the story: she'd met some bloke and didn't want him or the child. I was the only person she could think of that would support her as she went through the abortion. Not thinking too much about it, I said that I would go with her, and I did.

As a young Christian, the rights or wrongs of the issue of abortion didn't enter my mind. Suffice to say that when it was over I was quite happy never to see Donna again. But a few months later she called, wanting to see me. It was then that I knew that I had to make it very clear that I not only had no feelings for her, but I never wanted to see her again. Even though I felt this might come across as a bit brutal, I knew that I had to totally cut all links with Donna once and for all. So when we met, I looked her in the eye and said, firmly, 'Donna, it's over between us. Finished.' And a huge weight fell off me. I was released from any hold she might have had over me. I thanked God for giving me the strength to be able to say what I did, and mean it.

Jacqui was never far from my thoughts. Sitting alone gluing bits of wood together, I thought over and over again at what a fool I had been to turn my back on my wonderful married, family life – for what? Drugs, drink, sex and lust, which nearly destroyed me. Right now, sitting in my old bedroom, I murmured, 'Thank you, Lord, for taking me out of that lifestyle and giving me hope.'

I had been phoning and meeting with Jacqui for a while. I knew that we couldn't pick up where we'd left off, but I was hoping that somehow God would allow us to have a new beginning, something that would be better than what we'd had before. My confidence was high concerning our relationship simply because we both had Jesus. There was no way that I felt Jacqui would have entertained me for a second if we hadn't both by then made a commitment to the Lord. My calling out to God was to save me and take me out of the mess I had made of my life. Jacqui around the same time had called out to God to comfort her because of the pain and heartache I had caused her and the children. I was learning that God was in the business of reconciliation. First to himself, and then to each other. I believe that any broken relationship, when given over to Jesus can be restored – when a person has made the choice to let Jesus into their life and take over.

Jacqui had to seek God to give her the strength to forgive me. She knew that women whose husbands had treated them as I had treated her would have allowed bitterness and unforgiveness to consume them. Jacqui didn't want the heavy burden of negative emotions clogging up her life; she wanted to be free, and she made the choice of forgiving me. I, on the other hand, was ravaged by guilt. Memories of what I had said and done would plague me, and I feared that Jacqui would not want me. Time and time again I had to pray, asking God to help me so that I could at least have rest in my mind. And God was good, not only in causing me and Jacqui to become good friends, but in getting our marriage back on track – in fact, on 1 August 1993 we were remarried.

But it didn't happen overnight. Even when we were living together as man and wife, I still had to seek after God through prayer and Bible study and Christian counselling that he would make me the man *he* wanted me to be, so that Jacqui could see that I had changed and was able to deal with situations differently, that she could trust and rely on me and not get her heart broken all over again. This was very important to me and I worked hard to maintain integrity. There were times when I did make a hash of things but the Lord was there for me to put me right again.

Married life was going well, but work wasn't. It was getting increasingly hard for me to be a Christian within an environment that was depraved and immoral. Before I knew Christ, I felt at one with the traders and workers, but now it sickened me – the lying, stealing, violence, the cesspit of humanity that surrounded me each and every day. It was as though I had had a blindfold removed from my eyes and I was really seeing the market for what it was.

Scouring the local paper's job section I spied a job for a trade foreman with a local building company. The salary was twenty grand a year, and it was something I could easily do – I had been in the building trade most of my life prior to being a debt collector.

I went for the interview and as the guy read through my CV I could tell that he was quite impressed.

'Would you come back for a second interview and meet the boss?' he said. 'I think I might have something else for you, something better.'

I had been disciplining myself to never make decisions without first talking them over with the Lord. My constant anguish with the debt collecting had resulted in the Lord opening the way for me to get this interview. More was to come. At the second interview I met the boss, and he offered me the position of assistant to the director on a new contract with Wandsworth council. The starting salary was £37,000, plus a car. This job was truly from the Lord and no one could tell me otherwise. It was too fantastic to be true!

I was eager to start, but soon the job took over my life – and it seemed no different to the environment I'd just left behind as a debt collector. Greed, aggression and anger were the driving forces behind the work. Now, I was back asking God for help.

Early one afternoon, the owner of the company paid his workers a visit. He screamed, shouted, cursed and berated everyone, including the director and me. Not wanting to retaliate as I would have done in the past, I resigned. The owner didn't want me to leave. He gave me twenty quid and told me to go to the café across the road to think about what I was doing. I went home. I knew the job was not for me. Within two or three days, the director visited me. He asked for the car keys, told me that they had lost the contract and there was now no longer any work for me anyway, and gave me five grand as payment in lieu. I had to praise the Lord! I could clearly see that God had not given up on me. He was teaching me a lesson that life wasn't about chasing money.

Shortly afterwards, a Christian guy at my church offered me a job. The salary was £20,000. God was truly looking after me.

7

JOINING TOUGH TALK

Life with Jacqui and my kids was sweet; my job was going well. I constantly marvelled at how the Lord had taken me from a deep pit of despair and self-destruction to a clean, wholesome family life.

Early in my Christian life, I was asked to share my testimony about how I became a Christian, and what God had done for me. I had been to a few youth meetings where I'd spoken about my experiences, and lifted some weights. I was interested in hearing about how God had changed other men's lives and I began to attend some Full Gospel Business Men's Fellowship International (FGBMFI) breakfast meetings. I arrived late at one such meeting, one Saturday morning in the West End of London, and found the only vacant seat out of 500! As I sat down I turned to the guy next to me.

'You look like you've done some training,' I said.

'Yeah, I have.' He shrugged. 'I'm Ian. Ian McDowall.'

I introduced myself. 'You look like you work out in the gym,' I said as I glanced at his broad shoulders.

'I would say the same about you!' Ian laughed. 'I'm a bodybuilder. And you?'

'I'm a powerlifter. I've been lifting for a few years now.'

He nodded. 'Since I've become a Christian, I've been speaking at different churches, sharing my faith in Jesus Christ. I lift a few weights as well as a sort of backdrop. It's amazing how many people are fascinated with my life story, especially when they see me lifting! I've had so many bookings that I thought it best to give the work a name, so I've called it Tough Talk.'

I was intrigued. 'Tough Talk?'

'Yeah. I was visiting a church in north London, and the minister there told the congregation to come and listen to a "Tough Talk" because life can be tough, and we all know that's true. Who could argue with that?'

I grinned. We exchanged phone details. Truthfully, I was not really expecting to hear from Ian again, but a few weeks later he contacted me and asked if I would like to go with him to a chapel service at a prison and give my testimony.

On the way to the prison, he told me more about Tough Talk.

'I found it hard at first to go to church,' he said. 'As a man's man, if you like, it was difficult for me to walk through the church doors. But as time went on I kept going, and now it isn't a problem for me. Anyway, I can understand why men may find it hard to visit a church, so I'll take the gospel to them! God has become so real to me I feel compelled to tell others the truth of the Bible.'

Ian explained that the Bible says: '. . . sin entered the world through one man, and death through sin, and in this way death came to all men, because all sinned' (Rom. 5:12). Then he went on, from the book of Colossians: 'For he has rescued us from the dominion of darkness and brought us into the kingdom of the Son he loves, in whom we have redemption, the forgiveness of sins' (Col. 1:13,14).

'So Arthur,' he said, 'it's clear that you don't have to be as bad as you and me! We've *all* sinned, and it's only through Jesus' blood we have forgiveness.' He paused for a minute. 'The thing is, mate, if we put up a poster saying "Arthur White – Preaching On The Blood Of Jesus", who's going to turn up? But if the poster reads: "Come Hear Some Hardcore Stories and See Some Big Weights Lifted", this'll probably get more interest. See?'

Nodding my head I said, 'You're probably right.'

On the journey home, I really gave some serious thought to what Ian had said. I felt I wanted to be part of Tough Talk, which at this time had been running for a couple of years.

◆　　◆　　◆

In joining Tough Talk, I was with a bunch of guys with similar backgrounds and experiences. There was Adam McMillan, ex-car thief, Marcus Williams, ex-body-builder, and Steve Johnson, ex-hard man and alcoholic. Previously, I had been speaking on my own, but now I was with like-minded men, travelling the country, sharing with people what God had done in our lives.

Ian had received an invitation for Tough Talk to go to New York, USA. Up until this point we had spoken to a few hundred people at many different meetings throughout the United Kingdom. New York would be a new door that God was opening for us. It was an exciting challenge. Things began to move fast as we prepared to go to America.

And so, in 1999, we found ourselves at Christ Tabernacle, in Queens, New York. With 1,200 seats, it was an overwhelming experience. Ian gave the invitation for people to receive Jesus, and hundreds came forward. It was great to see God touching people's hearts.

As we were packing away our stuff, getting ready to leave, the leader of the church rushed up and told us that a young guy who was a local gang member had been planning to do a drive-by shooting that evening. Passing the church, he'd felt compelled to come in, and when he'd heard the message of Christ, he'd responded and come forward. Whilst praying with one of the church members, he had related his story and his intentions, and handed over his gun, saying, 'If God can change these men, he can change me.'

It hadn't been too long before this that I'd seen and experienced pain and hurt in my own life, and in the lives of those around me. Now, as a Christian, I was seeing joy and hope as people's lives were transformed.

As a group, we had never had any definite plans about what Tough Talk was to do, or where we were to go. But after this meeting in New York, it was obvious that God had a plan for us as a team, and as individuals. We entered the new millennium, and Tough Talk became a registered Christian charity, of which I am a Trustee.

◆   ◆   ◆

I'd been experiencing a yearning to return to the gym. For many years gym training had been a big part of my life. And besides, I wanted to get fit again. Jacqui was all for it; I think she could sense my restlessness for the challenge of training.

Entering my old gym the familiar sounds and smells were overwhelming. It was good to be back. There were a few faces that I didn't recognize, but on the whole it was as though I had never been away.

Coming out of the changing rooms, I bumped into a guy I knew named Tony. He was a big man, about six foot four, pure muscle. As I shook his hand, he passed a package to me. 'This'll give you a kick-start, put you back on track.' He walked off.

I opened the envelope. Four syringes and a bottle of testosterone. My stomach flipped as memories of my past dependency on steroids came flooding back. I dropped the package straight in the bin. Throughout my training session the temptation to take the drug was strong. I trained hard, trying to push the thought of the drug and its effect out of my mind.

Later, standing in the car park, I felt so elated by the session that I looked up into the sky and asked God if I should compete again. In a way it was a dangerous question, as my fall from the normal to the violent life, of which drugs was a great part, began in the gym and competition. My mind was racing. Then peace began to settle over me, and I heard the Lord: '*All that you were, all that you are, and all that you will be is for me.*' My interpretation of that statement was: although I had done a lot of things that were wrong, he could use what I was doing now – and he could also use my thoughts about what I would do in the future. That settled the issue for me. I would now start putting out feelers to get me back on the competition scene.

I think the church people I looked to for wise counsel and advice, and even Jacqui, were pleased that I was going to resume my lifting career. But they also feared that I might get dragged back into drug-taking, and allow the powerlifting to become a kind of god to me again and cause me to fall away from the Lord. It was now up to me to ensure, with God's help, that I would have the strength to stand strong. I found that being with Tough Talk gave me plenty of the kind of support I needed.

I stepped up my training regime to four times a week. The buzz I was getting as a new Christian and training without the aid of drugs was exhilarating. At the gym I knew most of the guys were taking something to enhance their performance, but not me. Many of them would rib me and say, 'Hey, Arthur, what are you taking? I could do with some of that.'

I would laugh. 'What I'm on you can have for free!'

Since I had started back training, I'd amazed myself. My strength and vitality came flooding back with such force I knew that I would soon be ready to compete. Jacqui was very supportive. We prayed together, and she always included my training and competitions, that God would guide and protect me.

In 2000 I entered the British Powerlifting Championships. It felt great to be performing in front of a crowd. I had no fear, just a great feeling of expectation that God would enable me to do well. I did more than well – I won. I was the British Champion and I was selected to be part of the British powerlifting team that would represent England in the European Championships in Slovakia.

I realized that most of the British team would not know Christ as their Saviour. So I made it my business to have Christian literature and leaflets to give away. I was prepared not just physically, but spiritually, to compete. I was now training and competing drug-free and free in my spirit with an inner strength that came from God.

My status as a powerlifter after my success at the European Championships caused me to be ranked second in Europe and third in the world. God helped me to be physically fitter, and I won more titles as a Christian than at any other period in my life.

I was very eager to share my faith, and I used every opportunity. Before I was a Christian I wore shirts that represented Britain; now I was also representing God, so

all the shirts that I competed in had been printed with a
Scripture verse on the sleeve. At the World Championships in Canada, I was getting my kit checked out to
ensure that I was fulfilling the competition require-
ments, when a Japanese referee saw the Scripture verses.

'No, no!' He shook his head. He couldn't read
English, but anything other than the national flag was
prohibited. Next to him was a Canadian referee. He
glanced at the Bible verses and spoke quickly to the
Japanese man, telling him my shirts would be allowed.
The Canadian referee was a Christian.

'Are you born again, Arthur?' he smiled.

'Yes,' I said. 'I am.'

'Praise the Lord, Arthur!'

It was a great feeling to know that even though I was
thousands of miles from home, the Lord had his people
everywhere. I used every opportunity presented to me;
the new titles were opening more doors for the work of
Tough Talk.

Now that I was a Christian I had a new circle of friends.
Church was still a puzzle to me at times, though. It seemed
that everyone was happy and joyful, feeling comfortable
with all that Christian activity. It took me a long time to
completely immerse myself and feel at home. I still kept in
contact with some of my old mates, and every one of them
knew that I was a Christian. Even if I didn't tell them at
first, they could see my conduct had changed and would
comment on it. But there were many people I had to totally disassociate myself from, as I knew that being close to
them could have a very negative effect on me. Most of the
guys in Tough Talk had struggles of their own. But sharing our faults and shortcomings with each other and praying together helped me during those difficult times.

There was absolutely nothing of my past that I
missed. That period of my life was a closed book, and all

I could see ahead was my new life in Christ. Unfortunately, however, your past has a tendency to intrude into your present life without any warning.

Jacqui and I were quietly relaxing at home one evening when the phone rang. Casually, I answered it.

'Hello, Arthur.'

Donna! I froze as I heard her voice. Jacqui must have seen the expression on my face, because she whispered, 'Who is it?'

I looked at her. Should I lie to her, or should I tell her the truth?

'It's Donna,' I said.

She nodded. I was thankful that both Jacqui and I were saved, and that God had healed our relationship to such an extent that she could trust me.

'Yeah, what's up?' I said into the receiver.

Donna started to tell me about the flat we still jointly owned. She was in arrears with the mortgage and she had received a summons to appear in court. Throughout the conversation, I was relating it back word for word to Jacqui. Donna told me that she was phoning me just to let me know the circumstances concerning the flat in case the court contacted me.

'Tell her,' said Jacqui, 'whatever happens, not to lose the flat.'

I knew where Jacqui was going with this line of thinking; we would take over the flat, then sell it and hopefully make some money on it. But God had other plans.

I never heard from Donna again. But I did hear from the building society that held the mortgage. The flat had been finally repossessed and sold but there was a shortfall. Because they couldn't find Donna, and both our names were on the deeds, they were coming after me for the outstanding monies. When I first read the letter, I didn't feel too put out by the total sum of £4,980. I didn't have the money, but Jacqui agreed that we could add it to our present mortgage. But when I reread the letter I was shocked. Somehow the £4,980 had mushroomed into £49,800! My jaw dropped. Jacqui and I were speechless. How in the world were we going to pay this off?

Clearly, this situation was the result of unrighteous living. It may sound a bit sanctimonious to say this, but the fact was I'd been in an adulterous relationship, taking illegal drugs, earning illegal money, and living a crazed, violent lifestyle. I had lied to get the mortgage in the first place, and the money spent on the upkeep of the flat had been illegally gained. I was learning that we all have to bear the consequences of our actions!

My solicitors advised me to allow them to present my case to the court in such a way that would exonerate me. But I told them to do the 'right' thing, and we would go from there. And now I learnt about God's mercy. Even though the whole flat issue was a bad thing, because I had confessed everything to God, I knew that somehow he would turn things around for me. When I next heard from the solicitors they told me that the building society had agreed that I had to pay £5,000 instead of the huge sum of nearly £50,000! Jacqui and I really praised God for his goodness to us.

8

LIVING THE LIFE

God had so transformed me that I was amazed. I'd changed from being a violent, drug-taking person to one who was interested in people, loved my wife and family, and was at peace with myself. Yet, the old demons refused to let me go.

Over one Christmas period I had been doing some Christmas shopping and had unknowingly parked in someone's private space. Just as I was climbing into my car, the man whose space it was charged out to me. His face and eyes were red – he'd been drinking. I tried to ignore the guy. He threatened me. I controlled myself and refused to rise to the bait. Then he got in his car and parked across the back of mine, blocking me in. By now, my stomach was churning; it was only God's power that was restraining me. But it was getting very hard for me.

If I had got out of the car, this guy and I would have had a fight, and I knew he would have been badly hurt. I started my car, mounted the pavement and drove off. Looking in the rear-view mirror, I could see that my getting the better of him had made him really angry. As I drove, I too began to seethe. 'This guy is out of order. How dare he speak to me like that?'

I turned my car around. In my heart I knew what I was doing was wrong; God gently touched me, and I turned back and headed for home. But anger was still stirring my blood to boiling point. I turned my car again, and this time I put my foot down, pushing all sensible reasoning out of my mind. This guy needed to be taught a lesson.

Suddenly, I felt a strong urge to pull the car over. My breathing was shallow. God was speaking to me: *'Arthur, if you go back, what's going to happen? You could get hurt, the man could get hurt. One of you could die. The police might get involved. You claim to be a changed man, and here you are, wanting to hurt this guy. What witness would this be?'*

I was rebuked. I now felt ashamed of my attitude. When I was working the doors, I had been spat at, sworn at, shot and stabbed, and I was able to walk away from it all. So in comparison this was trivial, and I had too much to lose.

I let it go, and instantly I was flooded with God's peace and the assurance of his love.

♦   ♦   ♦

'Will you take this man to be your lawful wedded husband?'

Emma beamed. 'I do.'

Standing in the church in 2002 as my precious daughter said her vows brought so much joy to my heart. God had been so good to me, despite my terrible past. Throughout the wedding ceremony and celebrations, I thought about the place where God had found me, and what had happened since. If I had not responded to Jesus' invitation to accept him as my Saviour, I knew for sure that I would either be lying in some gutter, in prison, or dead. Instead, I was with my family, experiencing love, unity and care.

Most people have no real notion of what it means to belong to Jesus. Any idea they do have is usually negative. I was no different. But now that I know the benefits of being a Christian I wished that I had committed my life to God years ago. Emma had been instrumental in both Jacqui and I coming to know Jesus, and she'd had the same effect on her husband. The day flashed by so fast I was saddened when it was all over.

Twenty-four hours later I was on a plane bound for Argentina to compete in the World Championships Powerlifting event. Being the British and European Champion of 2002 I was pretty confident that I would do well, but I wasn't taking any chances. I was in continual communication with my Father all the way.

I never went out of my way to share my faith with people, yet God always caused people to cross my path so that I could tell them how good he is. I had many such meetings with an assortment of people in Argentina. I was now working full-time for Tough Talk, so when asked what I did for a living, it made it easier to share the gospel.

The athletes that were competing alongside me were a mixed bunch of guys. Initially, most of them kept themselves to themselves. I did the same, as I needed to focus on what I had to do; socializing was a distraction.

My event was drawing to its finale. There were two Americans and I competing for the world title. My rivals would lift and gain first place, then I would lift and gain first – who was going to be the winner? Then one of the Americans injured his bicep muscle and could no longer compete. That left me and the other American. I was praying and asking for God's favour. A strange thought popped into my head: '*Go and pray for the injured guy.*' At first, I dismissed it. But the thought became so strong that I knew I had to obey God's leading. So I went to find the guy, very conscious that the minutes were ticking away to my next lift. He was in the warm-up area, surrounded by people who were all trying to ease his pain. I strode right up to him and, in front of everyone, asked if I could pray for him. Everybody looked at me. I had no time for niceties. I laid my hand on his arm and prayed.

A voice came over the Tannoy: 'The next lifter on the platform is Arthur White from Great Britain. You have one minute.'

'Amen!' I said, and hastily made my way to the platform. My heart was thumping and sweat bubbles popped across my forehead. There was no time for me to get psyched up, or anxious, or peaceful. I just had to lift and trust the Lord would be with me.

I won! I was the World Champion Powerlifter for 2002. On the plane home the next day, I wondered what the outcome would have been if I hadn't prayed for that guy. The question of obedience is an important one in the life of a Christian. I wondered if God's favour would have been on me if I hadn't obeyed.

The work of Tough Talk grew over the next few years. There were bigger meetings, and TV, radio and newspapers were all reporting the work of this team that was lifting weights and sharing life stories about Jesus Christ! Alongside this, I competed and continued to win many championships. God orchestrated for me to travel nationally and internationally, meeting many new people and making friends. Throughout this time, God revealed himself to me in ways that were beyond my hopes and dreams. My life was balancing out with a normality that others probably take for granted.

Our house in Loughton was very, very comfortable. It was filled with a lot of good memories that both Jacqui and I cherished, so it was a bit of a surprise when she suggested we do overseas missionary work. Still, I was up for a move. Through my adulterous, drug-crazed years I had wracked up quite a bit of debt which had increased our mortgage. I had estimated that in my life-time I would never be able to pay it off.

As we prayed and contemplated moving, I had reservations about where we could end up. We had visited Uganda a number of times, and I must admit I did tell God that much as I loved Africa, to spend the rest of my days living under a baking hot sun did not sit too well with me – but if that was God's plan for my life, I would do it.

Emma and her husband had left Essex and had moved to Cornwall. We had been to her house once, and truthfully I had never given Cornwall another thought.

Then, during a Tough Talk prayer meeting, a man who had little knowledge of our hearts' plans told me: 'God is saying that you will move – not to Africa, but to Cornwall. And the reason is more for Jacqui than for you.'

Straight away I knew this was right. Jacqui has been involved in short-term missionary work, guest-speaking at many women's meetings and working for a Christian organization. Since becoming a Christian, I had pretty much lived the life I wanted to live. God's grace – his unmerited favour – was on me and my family, and although things weren't perfect (Christianity doesn't mean that life is always a bed of roses!) they were generally going well.

Jacqui and I felt strongly that we had to move to Cornwall. We were both apprehensive because Cornwall was 'out in the sticks', and life would no longer have the energy and excitement of London and Essex. And how would it affect my involvement with Tough Talk? But of course, we were seeing our future through our own futile, limited mindsets. Cornwall was far beyond our expectations; we both instantly felt at home. And although 300 miles from Essex, modern-day communications, motorways, trains and planes meant the distance did not hinder my continued work with Tough Talk.

Emma and her husband, David, had purchased a large house with a barn attached which I converted into a two-bedroom house. My daughter and son-in-law were already established in a church, and I thought life couldn't get any better. Then in 2005 Jacqui and I became grandparents to Katie, Emma's first child. More good news came when my son, James, moved to Cornwall to be close to us. My days were filled to the brim with God's goodness.

◆　◆　◆

The following years had me still on the powerlifting circuit. I was winning titles and travelling up to London and all over the country as God opened more doors for Tough Talk, especially in prisons, where we'd tell inmates that the best thing they could ever do would be to surrender their lives to Jesus, and turn from the way they were living.

The years that I had spent working in the building trade, training in the gym and powerlifting had taken its toll on my body. I always had some pain, especially in my legs and knees, but what I began to experience in 2008 was something totally different. In January of that year, both my knee joints collapsed. Previous operations on my legs had resulted in having 7½ centimetres sawn off, reducing my height but straightening my legs. These operations enabled me to carry on lifting. But now I needed new knee joints.

I had been asking Jesus to heal me. I'd read about Jesus healing the sick in the Bible, and had talked with people who were either healed themselves or knew of others who had been. So I was confident that I would be healed; I was hoping for a kind of biblical miracle. But that didn't happen.

During my time in hospital, my second granddaughter, Sarah, was born. But along with that happy event came bad news. I discovered I had a heart problem. Forty years in the building trade and thirty years as a competitive lifter found me in a hospital bed, suffering. Much of it was the result of everyday living, but everything has a price – the illegal drug-taking had damaged my heart.

I'd been proud of the fact that I had been able to earn a living, provide for my family and compete on the international stage. But sitting at home with my Bible on my lap I felt like a useless old man. I had lost the strength in my hands, which stopped me working and lifting. My daily routine became a chore. I was struggling to put my socks on! Still, I believed that God's Word is infallible, and that he had promised never to leave or forsake me (Heb. 13:5). Before I was even born, God had planned all my days (Ps. 139:16). When I was wallowing in filth and degradation, God saw and knew. He never left me, but watched over me and saw the mess I got myself in, and when I cried out to him, he took me out of it, turned me around and gave me a fresh start.

Over a period of time, my heart slowly healed. The medication will come to an end soon and I'll be totally restored. My inner and physical strength has come back to me and I am able to do most of the things I did before, except for powerlifting – although at my age, I don't particularly want to do that any more! God is using me in different ways to spread the truth of the gospel. Although I no longer lift weights, the Tough Talk team has grown in numbers. So I continue to share my story alongside the weightlifting, encouraging people to give their lives to Jesus. God is doing a new thing for me at an age when people usually think it's time for them to wind down and wait for death. But I feel like a child looking forward to my life ahead, because of my Father's caring love; I know he wants the best for me. And this isn't for me alone – it's for everyone who decides to make God the head of their life, male or female, young or old, rich or poor, black or white.

I have made choices in my life, some bad, and some good. But the best choice I have ever made was to choose Jesus as my Saviour.

IAN
MCDOWALL

B.A.W.L.A. AWARD

Certificate of Record

This Diploma Certifies . . .

that on the __17th__ day of __April__ 19__82__

at __Munich, West Germany__

__Arthur White__

accomplished the undermentioned feat to the satisfaction of our duly appointed Representatives:—

__Two Hands Dead Lift – 380 Kg__

being a __British Senior__ Record in the __110 Kg__ Class

at a Body-weight of __109 · 4 Kg__

Signed __J.F.W. Moody__

Arthur's British and European deadlift record which still stands after 29 years

Arthur's winning deadlift, Munich 1982

World Championships, South Africa 2005
– Arthur's fourth world title

Ian training in 1988, showing the effects of steroids

Ian competing in the British Body Building Championships in 1989

Ian's baptism

Ian performing a squat

Ian and the Tough Talk team at Notting Hill Carnival

Ian with Arthur demonstrating the deadlift in Russia

Tough Talk at Kensington Temple, London

Tough Talk street outreach, East London

One of the team's many prison visits

Tough Talk at Alton Towers

Arthur speaking to soldiers at the British Army
barracks in Dusseldorf, Germany

The Tough Talk Team at HM Prison
Guernsey

1

PUMPING IT UP

'Ughhhhhhhhh!'

'C'mon, Ian, you can do it! One more rep,' shouted Tony.

Doing squats with a 400 lb barbell was like carrying the weight of the world on my shoulders. I wanted to stop.

'Don't give up Ian. Uppppp!' Tony bellowed in my ear. My whole body felt like a ton of lead. Every muscle was protesting against the onslaught of the gruelling regime I was putting my body through.

'Yes, 400 – you've done it!' said Tony, clapping me on the back.

I collapsed on the floor, drenched in sweat, but pleased that I had accomplished what I had set out to do.

Every day I gave myself goals to be achieved. No matter how hard or how difficult they were, I wouldn't feel good unless I reached them.

Slowly, I eased my five-foot-eight-inch, 17-stone bulk up off the floor, and made my way to the changing rooms.

The weather was bang on target for Christmas Eve – inside the gym and out. In the changing rooms, for as long as I had worked there, a window had been broken, and never repaired. Goose bumps appeared all over me like a rash.

'I reckon the only way that window is gonna get sorted is if I do it myself,' moaned Tony.

'Yeah, Allan's so tight, if you got it done, he'd probably dock your wages,' I laughed. Tony grinned; he knew exactly what I meant. Allan was the owner of the gym, and didn't much like spending money.

The hot shower enlivened me, the jets of water massaging my aching muscles.

'What d'ya say, Tony?' I could just about hear him, over the sound of the shower.

'I said,' yelled Tony, 'do you want me to get you the gear or not?'

My shower stopped, and I began to dry myself. The very question that Tony had asked me had been running around my mind for some time. The 'gear' that Tony was referring to was anabolic steroids.

I had already been taking an eight-week course of steroids in tablet form. From the time I'd started weight training, when I was about 14 years old, I had toyed with the idea of taking steroids, but I had resisted. Even though lots of people around me were chucking them down their throats or injecting them, I'd thought it was cheating. I took my first course because I was fed up with losing. Because I was so obsessed with my body and with winning, it was very hard for me to keep getting a knockback. I knew from the last competition that I had entered, and lost, that things would have to change. The very first tablet that I washed down with water, gave me an instant feeling of euphoria. Not because of the effect of the tablet, but because it gave me a psychological high in knowing the effect that the steroids would have on my appearance and performance in the long run.

The first competition that I entered after I started taking the steroids was in Portsmouth. It was a big affair for me. When my name was called out as the runner-up, I wanted to jump and yell, and scream out, 'Yes!' Instead, ever Mr Super Cool, I casually raised my hand, and sauntered towards the platform, where I collected the first of my many trophies.

Now, coming out of the shower, Tony's voice followed me as I walked to my locker.

'Well, do you or don't you?'

I pulled my jeans on, and answered: 'To tell you the truth, Tony, I feel ready to start taking some injectables, but it's the hundred quid, mate. I can't find it on Allan's wages.'

Tony grinned. 'You're right. We can just about afford a Big Mac on what he pays us.' Walking out of the gym into the cold early evening air, Tony and I laughed about our wages. But never one to lose the thread of a conversation, Tony continued to plague me about the gear.

'Look, I'd love to say to you, "Ian, here's a ton," but I know that you'll be wanting more. After all, I'm not a charity. Now, this brings me onto my next point . . .'

I knew what was coming.

'Why don't you do a shift for me tonight, eh?'

I began to shake my head. I had known Tony for about a year, and he was forever asking me to do some work as a bouncer with him. He worked day and night all over London, and was always on the lookout for help. The idea of working as a bouncer did not appeal to me at all. Why would I want to set myself up to get my head kicked in, or worse? And, if I had to defend myself – and I could, make no mistake about that – what if I ended up doing some guy a great deal of harm? I didn't fancy doing time because of it. No, that line of work was out, as far as I was concerned.

That was until Tony said the magic words: 'Double bubble, Ian.'

He grinned like Fagin, rubbing his fingers together.

I was tempted.

'Double bubble, you sure, Tony?' I tried not to seem too interested, but we were talking about seventy quid here, something that I couldn't sniff at.

'I'm telling you, mate, seventy smackeroonies.'

We walked towards the car park and got in to Tony's rust box of a car. There were no lights at the back of the gym. As Tony manoeuvred the car out to the road, my heart did a double somersault. I was scared that he would hit another vehicle. Tony didn't seem too bothered. When he approached the main road, and just swung out into the path of a juggernaut, I thought my time was up! My life was definitely worth more than seventy quid, and I wasn't too happy about putting my trust in Tony – because that is what I would have to do if I decided to take the job.

Tony was not one for giving up. We drove around the roundabout at Bow, east London, and headed for the bagel shop in Bethnal Green.

'Seventy quid could get you some decent gear, and get you set up for the next qualifier,' he continued.

My need to succeed was very strong: I badly wanted to win. As soon as that thought dropped into my mind, without thinking any more about it, I told Tony I would do a shift.

'Yes, my son, you've made the right move.' There was a lot of satisfaction in his voice.

We sat outside the bagel shop and demolished four salmon and cream cheese bagels, washing them down with a pint of cold milk. By ten minutes to seven, Tony and I were just up the road from the venue for the night – The White Hart pub, which was a pretty dilapidated establishment. Tony had said he wanted to show me something before we went in, so we walked round to the boot of his car. Tony fished around a bit. There was so much junk in his boot, I was surprised he could find anything.

'Here, grab a hold of this, Ian.'

I looked in horror as he handed me a wooden baseball bat. 'What's this for?'

'This is called self-preservation,' he replied.

'Nah, sorry, mate, I can't handle this. It's asking for aggro.'

'Don't panic. I guarantee we'll have no trouble tonight. But if a punter starts to get a bit excited, one rap from this will sort 'im out.'

Reluctantly, I followed Tony into the pub. He spoke to the landlord, and I just nodded to him. We then took up our posts, just outside the door. I had shoved the base-ball bat in the inside pocket of my leather jacket. Having it so close to my skin was not too reassuring. A quick glance at my watch told me that it was only 7.20 p.m. The night was still very, very young. The cold air pene-trated right through my clothing. It felt as though my body was seizing up. I shoved my hands deeper into my jacket pockets. Wrong move – my knuckles touched the baseball bat. I decided to keep both hands behind my back. As the people began to come in I wished, increas-ingly, that I'd stayed at home. Everyone looked as though they belonged to the land of giants; even the women seemed tall and threatening. And talk about mouthy! The ladies were so aggressive. Entry to the pub that night was by ticket only, and that's what caused a lot of the problems.

'Sorry love – no ticket. You can't come in.'

'You what?' A blonde wailing banshee shrieked back at me. 'I come 'ere every night, and you,' she pointed menacingly into my face, 'are not going to tell me other-wise.' She began to push against me, and the rest of her mates followed suit. This was hard for me because I had never hit a woman. But this one was asking for it.

'Listen, love, I said you can't come in.'

She wasn't having any of it. The shoving continued. Then a voice behind me said, 'It's all right, Ian, she's sweet. Let her in.' The group of women pushed past me, tutting and muttering. ''Ere Tony, where'd you get him from? A bit too full of himself if you ask me!'

'He's new, love, he's new,' Tony responded.

I felt a complete fool. If Tony had told me once, he'd told me a hundred times, admission by ticket only. I was only trying to do my job, and he had overruled me. It was like that for the next few hours. I would say no, they couldn't come in without a ticket, and Tony would over-rule me and let them in. The trouble was, for the major-ity of people, the pub was their regular haunt: they spent most nights having a drink there. Now that it was Christmas Eve, and tickets were required to get in, they felt that it was out of order.

All this aggravation didn't do a lot for my self-confi-dence. I must've looked, to the punters, like someone who could handle himself, and anyone else if need be. The truth of the matter was, I was more than a little apprehensive. There was a strong underlying feeling of fear that I had to suppress continually. There were so many 'what ifs' running through my brain: What if someone pulls a knife on me? What if a fight breaks out – will I run, or steam in? What if the Old Bill catches me with this bat?

Now and again my teeth would chatter and my body would shake. I didn't know whether it was because of the cold weather or fear. I looked over at Tony. He was involved in conversation with a few guys. He was laughing and joking with them. That was another concern I had – could I rely on him if it all kicked off? I was soon able to put that to the test.

By now it was 11.30 p.m. One more hour to go. It couldn't pass quickly enough for me. Tony had told me a while before that he was going to check the toilets. He seemed to be gone a long time. Stamping my feet and beating my hands together to keep my circulation going, I glanced over my shoulder and was horrified to see my worst nightmare coming true. In the centre of the pub, a group had gathered – something was happening. I didn't know what to do. Where was Tony?

Someone shouted to me. 'You're needed over there, mate. Looks like a bit of trouble!' Reluctantly, I waded through a sea of unyielding bodies.

'Get off me, yer dirty old man!' screamed a plump woman.

'You is my gal tonight!' slurred an elderly man.

The woman gazed around desperately. 'Help me, somebody!'

Taking a deep breath, I sized up the situation. The old guy was molesting the woman. He was short and skinny – I could handle him, I thought. I straightened myself up, and marched up to the man, and got him in a bear hug. With my strong arms restraining him, he didn't have a chance to break free. I pushed through the crowd, half-carrying the man, using his body as a battering ram to get through the door. The door flew open and I dropped him on the pavement.

'Now, clear off home!'

It felt good that I had managed to deal with the guy on my own. That feeling was short-lived. The guy was angry. He began to curse and shout, gesticulating wildly. I was cool and calm until the man came close to me. From nowhere, it seemed, he pulled a knife. The blade looked as if it was ten feet long. Automatically, I pulled out the baseball bat, and whacked the guy across the face. He fell in a crumpled heap to the ground, and I jumped on him, standing on the hand that held the knife. He yelled out in pain. Picking up the knife, I could see that it wasn't very big at all.

I had quickly put the bat back, which was just as well, as two policemen suddenly appeared and collared me. I had trouble explaining the situation to them. I don't think they believed me at first, but when they saw the knife, they let me go. They scraped the guy off the pavement and flung him in the back of their 'meat wagon', then drove off.

'What's happening, man?' asked Tony, slapping me on the back.

'What's happening, man?!' I shouted at him. 'Did you see that geezer with a blade? I nearly got *stabbed*, man! Where were you?'

'So what's your problem, eh? Good thing you had the bat.'

I didn't even bother to answer. Every worry that I had had about being a bouncer had come true that night. It just confirmed to me that this was going to be the first and the last time for me. Or so I thought.

♦   ♦   ♦

Early January was cold and frosty. The seventy quid was burning a hole in my pocket and I was eager to buy some steroids. The only drawback was Tony. After the fiasco at the pub, I wasn't keen to buy any gear from him. If he was unreliable at the job, how could I trust him to be my supplier? The problem of how I was going to get some gear was worrying me. It wasn't as if I could go to Boots and ask for it over the counter. I racked my brains to think of any people I knew who were into bodybuilding, people I could trust who might be able to help me. I came up with no one. Then, one night after work I was coming home on the bus when some guy came upstairs, where I was sitting, and sat across the aisle to me. At the same time, we looked at each other, and realized that we knew each other.

'Ian! All right, mate?'

Sam had been my first training partner. Boxing had been the thing that had got me into a gym when I was 14. Coming from Forest Gate and Ilford, in east London, I would travel all the way to Dagenham Boys' Club to train as a boxer. I was inspired by *Rocky*, the movie, and I thought that I could give Sylvester Stallone a run for his money. From the time I started weight training to help develop strength for boxing, I began to lose interest in the sport, and major more on developing my body. It was a wonderful thing to see my muscles blow up and curve and shape, causing my body to look good.

My mum was amused by it all. 'Look at the state of your body. You look like the Michelin man.'

She would walk around the room, pretending to be me, pulling faces. This was particularly funny because Mum had long blonde hair and model looks. My older brother thought I was a bit of a nutcase and took no notice of me. Jason, my younger brother, looked up to me, and even started doing some weights himself. Sadly, my dad was not around. The last time I had heard from him was when I was about 6. He'd emigrated to Australia, and had sent me a boomerang.

'So, where are you training now, Ian?' Sam asked.

'I'm still down at Allan's.'

Sam laughed. He knew Allan.

'How's Tony? Is he still selling the gear?'

This was a great opener for me. I had been wondering how I could broach the subject of steroids. As Sam had come right out with it himself, I launched straight in with, 'I think he's still dealing, but . . . eh, do you still sell a bit yourself?'

'Yeah, why – you interested?'

I told him that I was. 'The only thing is,' I said, 'I don't know how to inject myself.'

Sam nodded at me. 'No problem, mate. Look, I'll sort you out. Everything you need, I can supply.' He pulled a piece of paper and a stubby pencil out of his jacket pocket and wrote something down. He handed the paper to me. 'This is my number. Give us a bell, say . . .' he pondered for a moment, 'say in a couple of days, and I'll get it sorted for you.'

I was well pleased. It was a good thing I looked up, otherwise I would have missed my stop. Walking down the road, I thought that I was very lucky to have met up with Sam. Now my life could go in the direction that I wanted it to. I had seen the results of steroids, and I was confident that this was the way forward for me. For the next couple of days, I poured over the pages of *Beef It* and *Arnold's Education of Bodybuilders* magazines. I wanted to emulate the guys I saw in the photos. Their gleaming, well-honed muscles were what I hankered after. I knew that once I started injecting, my body would soon look like theirs.

Sam didn't live too far from me, and we had arranged to meet in the chip shop. We joked and laughed from the time we met until we entered his house. His mum was in. I said hello to her, then Sam quickly took me upstairs to his bedroom. We quickly demolished the saveloy and chips and washed it down with Coke. By now, I was feeling a bit uncomfortable. I have never been too fond of needles. But I was impressed with the way that Sam carried out the operation. First, he washed his hands. Then, he took out the syringe and needle from their sterile packs. He stuck the needle into the bottle, and drew up the liquid. Once the syringe barrel was full, he flicked the barrel to dispel all the air bubbles. He told me that he had to get rid of all the bubbles, otherwise, if he injected them into my body, I could end up with a heart attack, a stroke, or even dead. I was very nervous. It wouldn't have taken much for me to tell him to forget the whole thing. But I knew I had to go through with it if wanted to achieve my dream.

'Now, hold still, Ian,' said Sam.

I gripped the back of a chair tightly. Sam was giving me a lecture.

'I've got to stick the needle in the right place, Ian. You see this muscle here?' He pointed to the top part of my bottom. 'Very close to it is the sciatic nerve. One wrong jab and you're history, mate. You'll spend the rest of your days looking at life from a wheelchair, getting a disabled pension.'

My knees almost buckled with fear. Sam had instructed me to place one leg behind the other so that the muscle to be injected was relaxed. I felt so weak I wanted to sit down. Clenching my teeth, I said, 'Just do it, Sam, just do it!'

I sat down immediately afterwards. I felt drained, not because of the effect of the injection, but because of the whole scenario leading up to it. But it wasn't long before I started to feel myself again.

'Right,' said Sam, 'see you in a couple of days for the next lot.'

I thanked him and went home.

By the third time, I was injecting myself. I really didn't want to, but I knew that I had to if I wanted to achieve my goal. Sam taught me, stage by stage, how to correctly draw up the liquid in the syringe and aim the needle. It wasn't as bad as I thought it would be. Once I had done it once, I knew that it wasn't going to be too hard.

It took a couple of weeks to work, but it increased my body weight and strength. The downside of steroid-taking for me was losing my peace of mind. I had heard so many horror stories of people taking steroids and having massive heart attacks, liver or kidney failure, or just dropping dead, that I couldn't relax. But I continued to take them.

The twelve-week course was soon up and I had a break of four weeks. I was training twice a day, seven days a week. I recuperated so quickly from each workout that I was able to train frequently. The British Bodybuilding Championships were to be held in November 1986, and the qualifiers were monthly until then. I had decided to compete in the October trials, which meant that I needed to take another course of steroids as soon as possible. My confidence was increasing. Not only was I feeling very happy with the way my body was taking shape, but other people's comments made me feel good.

'Ian, c'mon, take your T-shirt off and show the boys what you look like,' said Wag, proudly. Wag was the owner of the gym I used to go to when I was younger. I had visited that day to do a bit of training. The compliments that the boys paid me made my ego swell.

The only cloud on the horizon was lack of money. During my twelve-week course of steroids, I'd been offered a couple of shifts doing some door work at a club in Woolwich called the Flamingo. I'd been reluctant, but the lure of £45 in my hand was enough to persuade me to take the job. I'd had to wear formal dress: dicky bow, white shirt and dinner jacket (bought in an Oxfam shop).

A guy who trained in the gym in Bow told me that the Ilford Palais was in need of doormen. I thought about it for a bit and realized that it was the only way for me to earn quick, easy money. So I went to see Joe, the head doorman at the Palais, and he gave me the job. The pay wasn't great, but I couldn't afford to turn it down. I told Joe about the job I did in Woolwich.

'Sorry mate, there's no way that I can match £45 – £30, that's it.'

'Well, OK, then,' I said. 'If you can give me five nights, I'll do it.'

He agreed.

My girlfriend, Val – who was my mate Marcus's sister – wasn't happy.

'What do you mean, you're gonna do five nights a week? What about me?' she shouted. 'This relationship's all about you, you, you. You're in the gym in the day, and now you're going to be at the Palais at night. What's the point of us dating, eh, Ian? What is the point?'

Staring into her angry face, I knew I had to choose my words carefully.

'Well, the thing is, Val, I'm thinking about you. I'm doing this for us. Just think, when I'm a pro and I'm on top, I'll be earning big bucks. You'll never want for anything. You can shop till you drop, then.'

She went quiet, and then she said, 'We'll see.'

The truth of the matter was, I was obsessed with bodybuilding and winning; I was obsessed with myself. Having a girlfriend was high on my list of priorities, but the number one spot belonged to me. Now I was in a position to go as far as I could, I was determined not only to be good, but to be the best!

2

JAMAICA

'Quick, upstairs, in the bar!' shouted Joe.

The panic button had sounded. There was trouble!

Tearing through the reception area, I braced myself for what lay ahead. Bashing into the double doors, which swung open, I turned left and bounded up the staircase. There was no time to politely ask people to move aside; my elbows did the talking for me.

'Out the way!' I yelled. Punters were spilling their drinks and choking on their cigarettes.

A couple of weeks had gone by, and I had more or less settled into my new job. It was strange how quickly I had become acclimatized to the environment of the Palais. It was the lure of the money that had made me take the job of doorman in the first place. I just thought that I would have to grit my teeth and bear it. But soon I found myself quite liking it, and all that went with it – even the violence.

I soon spotted the problem. A semicircle of people had gathered near to the bar. In the middle, there was some violent activity going on. As I got closer, I heard a blood-curdling scream: 'Get your hands off me!'

By now, there were quite a few other doormen who had also responded to the call. Two girls were bent low, trying to tear out the roots of each other's hair. I thought it was awful; the fact that two women were fighting was bad enough, but it was the way they were mauling each other that seemed terrible. I charged in, and grabbed the girl nearest to me. Yanking her away from her opponent wasn't easy; it took all my strength. I had my arms around the girl's waist, my plan being to get her as far away from the scene as possible. But the other woman had a gang of mates with her, who were just as ferocious and hungry for blood as she was. They encircled both the girl and me, and began to attack both of us.

'Let me get her!'

'I'm gonna kill you!'

A leg seemed to swing from out of nowhere. A very high-heeled shoe was attached to it. The foot caught the girl I was holding fully in the face, connecting with her nose. Blood began to gush out, like a waterfall. The sight of blood seemed to incite the pack of women, who were like baying wolves. Even as I was half-carrying, half-dragging the girl down the stairs, these crazy women were still attacking us. A high-heeled shoe was repeatedly being hammered into my back – and it hurt – but there wasn't anything that I could do.

I eventually managed to get her into the ladies' loo. She was hysterical. The poor girl was covered in blood – her hair, her clothes, everything. The other women were still trying to get to her and were kicking at the door, so I leaned hard against it. Finally, when the other doorman had got rid of them, I brought the girl out, got her into a cab, and off she went. What a shift!

Later that night, at home, as I cleaned the blood off my clothes, I wondered if it was all worth it. Yes, I needed the money badly, but perhaps there was another way of earning it. My body ached from the punches and kicks I had received from the girls. I was sore all over.

Sometimes, I wished that I had been born with some sort of talent – been an artist, or even a professional footballer. That way, I could have pursued my dream of being 'somebody' without resorting to artificial help. That, of course, was my true aim; the thought of living my whole life as a 'nobody' was depressing. I had to achieve *something* with my life. That was the whole point. It was my life, and I had to make good use of it.

I had to do better. I had to win. Where were the seeds of this obsessive mindset first sown? When I lived in Jamaica.

◆   ◆   ◆

Tom, my stepfather, was a vet. He married my mum when I was about 5 or 6 years old. Tom's temper was well known throughout the family. Whenever my mum and Tom started a fight, we children would disappear. There would be wild accusations, name-calling, then slaps and punches. Most of the fisticuffs would come from Mum; she gave Tom as good as she got. When we heard the front door slam, we kids knew that Tom had run out, and it was safe for us to come back.

Mum and Tom's relationship was precarious. There was no love in it, as far as I could see. Mum seemed to have no positive feelings for Tom and, from his behaviour, it seemed as though he had little fondness for Mum. But this was how it appeared from my viewpoint, as a child; couples who are violent to one another can still love each other – but to me, at that time, it seemed like a relationship filled with hatred.

As far as I can remember, Tom never showed me any affection. My two half-brothers (who were like full brothers to me) didn't fare any better with him. My heart was like ice towards Tom, and I expect the feeling was mutual, judging by his attitude towards me.

'You're as thick as two short planks. You'll never amount to anything.' These words revolved around my mind for years.

The Christmas that I was 12, my mum bought us some strange presents: snorkels, swimming goggles and flippers. My sister, brothers and I were puzzled. Then my mum dropped a bombshell.

'Get packed, kids. We're all off to live in Jamaica!'

There wasn't enough time to take in all that this would entail. I knew I'd really miss my friends, but it was wonderful to tell my teachers that I wouldn't be in school any longer, as I was emigrating.

Stepping off the plane at Montego Bay into 70°F was bliss. When we had left England, it was covered in snow. I knew, from my first few steps on Jamaican soil, that I was going to love it.

I was meant to go to high school, but for some reason it didn't happen. So, for a whole year, I didn't go to school at all. My education came through the experiences of life I gained during that year. I explored the island from coast to coast. We lived near Ocho Rios, which is famous because of Dunn's River waterfalls. I spent many of my days fishing and swimming. Some days were spent going up into the mountains with friends. Every day was long and lazy. Everyone had a machete, including me. It wasn't for violent purposes, just for everyday use: chopping down the bush as I went on my walkabouts; cutting open jelly coconuts so I could drink the juice. It made me feel grown up, carrying a machete.

Bob Marley was mega-popular, and wherever I went I would be sure to hear one of his songs being played. The food was fantastic: jerk chicken or pork, Ackee and salt fish, rice and peas, Jamaican patties, hard dough bread, buns and cheese.

In Jamaica I grew taller, and my skin became darker. I didn't cut my hair for a year. It grew long, and the sun bleached it blond. The local girls thought I was a novelty, and showed great interest in me. I spent my days on the beach, and my nights drinking Red Stripe beer.

To me, everything about Jamaica was great. It made me realize that there was more to life than I had been experiencing. It affected my future expectations, which had until then been very limited indeed. While my school friends at home would be talking about becoming a plumber's mate or a mechanic, I had made up my mind that I was going to be 'somebody'!

But we didn't stay in Jamaica. We returned to England.

Life after Jamaica was very depressing; driving through the streets of London, from Heathrow Airport, was a real downer. Everywhere was grey – grey skies; grey buildings; grey atmosphere. Even the people looked grey.

School was a nightmare. I hadn't been the best pupil before but now, after my Caribbean experience, I just couldn't settle in. My old school, Wanstead High, was full and so I had to go to another school. The nearest one was Fairlop Waters, two bus rides away.

From the first day, I had problems. Being a teenager isn't easy; the pressures of life seem to intensify, making simple things complicated. Depression wrapped itself around me like a second skin. I hated going to lessons, and it wasn't long before I started to have run-ins with the teachers.

I made a few friends, boys like me. We were the school bullies. It was not unusual for us to approach another boy and start fighting with him for no reason. Thumping someone for their dinner money was an everyday occurrence. In fact, my gang and I had a little racket going. We actually had a book with names, days and amounts that were due.

One boy was so terrified of us that he didn't come to school for a few weeks. When he finally did, his mother came too, and I was summoned to the head's office. Being a bit cocky, I wasn't too bothered about it. At first, the head told me what the boy had claimed, and then he gave me room to tell my side of the story. I spun him some yarn about not having enough money to get home from school because I had to change buses, and how I came from a big family, and anything else that flashed through my brain that sounded good. He not only believed my web of half-lies, but he said, 'Ian, if you have any more difficulties in the future, please come and see me.' What a joke!

As time went by, I hardly attended lessons; I could see no reason to go – I wasn't learning anything, so there seemed no point. I slid comfortably into truancy. Once we had got our quota of dinner money for the day, my mates and I would take off to a pet shop just off the high street. At the back of the shop was an amusement arcade, with fruit machines, Space Invaders and pool tables, which attracted young boys in similar situations – truants and general low-life. The smoky atmosphere was conducive to all manner of illegalities. By the time I reached 15, it seemed like a waste of time even attempting to go to school, so I left. All day, every day, was spent playing pool and arcade games.

At home, post-Jamaica was having an effect too. Mum and Tom's shaky relationship was virtually finished. What finally pushed it over the edge was when Tom's 'other woman' turned up on our doorstep. She was a professional limbo dancer, and Tom had started dating her in Jamaica. She was a very demanding woman. In her lilting West Indian accent she said to Mum, 'You have to all move out. I's come to take over yur house.'

After the initial shock, Mum snapped into action. She drew back her arm, balled her hand into a fist, and whacked the woman in the mouth. Then Mum shut the door. There was nothing more to be said. It was a while before Tom showed his face in our house again.

At 16 I had no qualifications, or any prospect of earning money. I knew that Tom had a lot of customers who avoided paying him, so I offered him my services as a debt collector. I started work right away.

My natural ability soon got me noticed. Stan was a debt collector, but on a far superior scale to me. He asked me if I wanted to earn some serious money. How could I resist! For £40 a day, I would accompany him on his travels around London. He would leave his van to pay a visit, and often returned carrying bundles of money. My job was to wait in the van with a baseball bat. If anything went off, I was meant to rush over to Stan's aid, and wield the bat across heads. It never happened, because Stan was a very persuasive man. And I was glad that my services weren't called upon – I wasn't sure if I had enough guts to go out there and help him.

♦　　♦　　♦

I soon realized that to continue working at the Ilford Palais and survive, I would need some tools of the trade. I purchased a knuckle-duster, a strip of heavy metal that sat across the knuckles of my right hand. It was a good investment – I was never without it.

There were six or seven fights most nights at the Palais. Monday nights were the worst. This was the night for the over-25s. Once, after a very eventful shift, I was glad to be going home. Ron, the other guy who was doing the shift with me, didn't live too far from where I was staying. At 3 a.m. there were no buses running and, as Ron didn't have any wheels, I would usually drop him home.

This particular night, we were driving along, chatting, when I noticed a car with glaring lights driving close to my bumper. It wasn't long before I realized that the car behind was following us. It eventually drew alongside, and then overtook us. As the car passed, I recognized the men in it. Earlier at the Palais, Ron and I had had to throw them out. They'd spent the remainder of our shift driving up and down past the Palais, pretending that their hands were guns, and that they were shooting us.

The car slowed to a halt, right in front of us.

'What we gonna do, Ian?' asked Ron.

'We're gonna get 'em,' I replied, grimly. 'Right now.'

It really annoyed me that somebody had the nerve to follow me home. I slipped on the knuckle-duster and leapt out of the car like Superman. The driver was just getting out as I reached their vehicle. I grabbed the door as he stood up, squashing him in it. I wasn't sure if he had a gun or whatever, and I wasn't going to give him a chance to use it. I began to pound on his face, and he screamed out in pain. Then he went quiet. I was holding him up, but as soon as I let the door go, he flopped down onto the ground. There was blood everywhere.

Meanwhile, Ron had wrenched a heavy screwdriver out of the other guy's hand, and was using it on him. This guy was still in the car, and he was taking a heavy battering.

'Ron, stop. That's enough. Let's go!' I shouted. I could see that if I had left Ron to his own devices, he could have killed the guy.

We drove off. I didn't take Ron straight home, but did a few detours, just in case we were being followed. We weren't. By the time I dropped Ron off, we were laughing about the night's events. Those guys had thought they were going to teach us a lesson, but we'd taught *them* a thing or two.

Later that night, as I was eating a bowl of cornflakes, Dean, the assistant manager of the Palais, called me. The two guys Ron and I had sorted out had been picked up by the police. They'd told the cops that two doormen from the Ilford Palais were responsible. The police went straight to the Palais with the guys, who picked out Dean as the perpetrator of the crime. Dean was arrested, but the police had to finally let him go. It would have been impossible for Dean to have been responsible for the guys' injuries; he was short and weighed about nine stone. I found this very amusing, and laughed all the more.

The money was now rolling in from my door work. I was taking steroids again, and I now needed to diet seriously if I wanted to win competitively. I also heard that an old training partner of mine, who was now a competitor, was using seventeen or eighteen different types of steroids. I was only taking two or three, so I decided to purchase more. Someone told me of a veterinary drug which was supposed to be powerful. At that time, I was living in a small, one-bedroom flat above Tom's surgery. When I was 17, going on 18, my mum had decided to head for the sunny shores of Clacton-on-Sea. I didn't want to leave London, so I'd stayed on alone in our empty house in Ilford for about six months without electricity, gas, water, or a phone. I'd slept on a mattress on the floorboards, with a carving knife under my pillow. I was able to shower at the gym, and use the microwave. Tom felt sorry for me and offered me the flat. That's how I became Tom's tenant.

I repaid Tom for his generosity by nipping down and helping myself from his store of drugs. I found a bottle of the substance I was looking for: on the label it read,

'Dosage: horses – 1 ml per week; bovine – 0.5 ml per week.' I started injecting 2 ml per day! The results were quickly noticeable. I ignored the fact that the label clearly stated that it wasn't to be administered to humans.

The combination of the steroids and my strict diet was getting to me: I was becoming increasingly aggressive.

3

TOP TOUCH

I was psyched up to the max. My determination to win the championships was high. My body had never looked so good: the dieting and training had really paid off. On the day of the championships I was feeling very positive.

At the weigh-in, I gave the other competitors the 'once over'. As I compared them to myself, I felt convinced that I was better. Some of my friends from the gym had accompanied me to the competition. They agreed that not only was I looking good but, if they were the judges, they wouldn't hesitate to pick me as the winner.

In the pre-judging section of the championships I did well, and I was confident that I would win. But I didn't, and it freaked me out. I came second, which just wasn't good enough for me. The winner was a guy who had won previous championships, and I think that the judges were swayed by a 'name' – well, that's what I told myself. Here I was, a year on from my last competition, tanked up to the hilt on steroids, and still I came second. My friends' words of comfort – 'You were robbed, Ian, you were robbed!' – did not pacify me. I wanted to win, and anything less was of no interest to me. I was fed up. Nothing seemed to be going my way, even though I was putting so much into it. I considered quitting.

After much soul-searching, I decided to give it another shot. I couldn't give up now, as I didn't know what else I could do. I felt as though I had backed myself into a corner, and there was only one course of action that I could take. I had big plans for myself, and I knew that the only person that could carry them out was me.

I was still dating Valerie. She was a patient, long-suffering girl. To add to my concerns, she started to press me about our relationship. I loved her, but I was totally wrapped up in my bodybuilding and the prestige and success that winning would bring. The main problem with our relationship was me. I was totally and utterly concerned with myself. Most of the money that I earned was spent on the essentials of living, and drugs. Bodybuilding is an expensive business. Food is a high priority: a chicken a day, lots of eggs, lots of vegetables, and fresh and tinned fish. Food supplements cost me a bomb – amino acids, liver tablets, protein and carbohydrate drinks – the list was endless.

Valerie, rightly, wanted more commitment from me. We decided, after Christmas 1987, to think seriously about where our relationship was going, and arranged to have a meal in a restaurant in Ilford to discuss it. For the previous two weeks, I had been taking a new steroid which was very, very strong, and toxic. It came in 50 mg tablets. By taking one a day, I immediately noticed the difference. My strength and weight increased quickly. But Sam, my supplier, advised me that one would not be enough; he told me that I should be on four a day.

'Just look at me, Ian,' he said.

I had to admit that Sam looked in fine form, but if I did as he suggested, it would mean that I was taking fourteen tablets and an injectable every day. Unfortunately, I took the four tablets on the day that Valerie and I were to have our 'in-depth' conversation about our relationship.

Throughout the day, I had been getting cramps and stomach pains, but I had ignored them. When the meal was served up, I was in severe pain, but I was trying to hold it together. Not wanting to let Val see that I was in a bad way, I gritted my teeth. I told her that we should get married. I had toyed with the idea, but actually thought that it would make more sense if we just lived together. But with the pain raging in my guts, I needed to curtail the conversation.

Valerie seemed shocked. 'Married? You sure, Ian?'

'Yeah, yeah, Val. Look, I love you, you love me, let's just do it.'

'When?'

'Soon. A couple of weeks' time.'

Slightly dazed, Val replied, 'What about arrangements, like where, and who's coming? And how much is it going to cost?'

The pain was intensifying.

'Don't worry. We can borrow some money from my mum, and maybe your dad. Let's just get the ball rolling, it'll sort itself out.'

I wanted to cut the talk and just go home. The pain was so bad, I had to excuse myself and go to the loo. I was drenched in sweat. The loos were conveniently empty. I threw myself onto the tiled floor and unbuttoned my jeans. My kidneys felt as though they had been kicked with hobnail boots. My whole body felt violated. It felt as though death was around the corner. This was it. At the tender age of 21, my life was over. All those plans of getting married were for nothing – I wouldn't be there! Lying sprawled out on the floor, I breathed deeply and wondered how Sam was able to take all those pills and live to tell the tale.

Fifteen minutes later, the pain had subsided. Slowly, I eased myself up, buttoned my jeans and went back out to Val.

'Where have you been?' she asked.

I played down my trauma. I didn't want Valerie to know what I had been up to. I only wanted her to see the good side of me. 'Oh,' I said, 'I had a bit of a stomach ache.'

The wedding day was set. We were married in church on 16 January 1988. Our honeymoon was spent in a hotel in Clacton. Within two days, I was in the hotel gym, working out. Valerie was shocked and disappointed that on our honeymoon I would rather be in the gym than spending the whole time with her.

This is how the early years of our marriage were. I saw more of gyms than I did our flat. It was a constant bone of contention between us. Valerie began to get on my case about earning 'proper' money – getting a job – but I didn't want to know. A regular job would not bring me what I was yearning for. I tried to reason with Val about my goals and ambitions, but she was having none of it. I was afraid of losing her, so I agreed to apply for a job as a fireman. I didn't get the position, which I was relieved about, but it brought home to me the seriousness of being a husband; it was loaded with responsibilities.

I worked out even harder. My need to win was growing by the day. I now had to prove to Valerie that training was a valid occupation.

The need to get more money was paramount. Sam introduced me to a guy who was a well-known supplier. I decided to go into partnership with him, but it didn't last. I then started dealing on my own. I was earning good money, but never let on to Valerie how much was slipping through my fingers. As the money was coming in, I was swallowing or injecting it away.

Around this time I was offered a job at Top Touch, a club in Dagenham. I took the job because its rate of pay was better than I was getting at the Palais. I was working with older guys, which I preferred. I was impressed with the way these guys presented themselves, in dinner jackets and ties, and they took a pride in their work. I felt as though I had taken a step up in life.

The other benefit for me in working at the club was that I was able to increase my clientele. There was a gym at the end of the road. Most of the members came to the club after working out. Some of the guys were really mouthy and flash. Working on the front door, we had to put up with a lot of nonsense. There was one particular guy who, when we got chatting, asked if I knew anyone who could get hold of some gear. I told him that I could sort him out with some stuff, and he became one of my regular punters for injectables. But I didn't like this guy. He irritated me, and bored me with his incessant chatting. He was too frightened to inject himself, so rather sheepishly asked if I could do it. He didn't realize it, but while he was babbling on about a load of rubbish, I was injecting him with an empty syringe barrel. After he paid me about a hundred quid, I would inject him, and send him on his way. He was happy, but in reality, he wasn't getting anything. I used the drug on myself!

Top Touch was known as a nightclub, but in reality it was a drinking man's club. Many of the punters were in their early thirties and beyond. Most of the time things were peaceful, but when something happened, it was a big affair. Barry and Gary, who worked with me at Top Touch, were twins. They reminded me of the Krays, in that they were not the sort of people that you would mess with: they could handle themselves.

One night Barry came down to the front door. 'Listen, guys, I think that something's gonna go off tonight. There's a crowd of "townies" upstairs, and I know they're gonna be up for it.'

He didn't have to say any more. Chris, the other guy on the door, and I knew what would be expected of us. My heart did a few flips. Excitement and fear, mingled with the rush of adrenaline, flooded my bloodstream. I slipped my hand into my pocket, and felt the reassuring cold metal of the knuckle-duster. A baseball bat was resting inside my jacket pocket. The 'fight or flight' mechanism kicked in. I was ready to go to war.

Five minutes later we were still downstairs, limbering up ready for the call. It came. Simon, who was Barry's stepson, worked the cloakroom. He shouted down to us: 'Ian, Chris! Quick, it's going off!'

We bounded up the stairs, taking them two at a time. Bursting in through the double doors, we saw a commotion around the bar area. Steaming through the dancing crowd, we approached the trouble. It was obvious that someone had taken a beating. One guy had blood coming out of his nose. Barry was holding him back, while Gary held onto his opponent. There were groups of men surrounding them. It looked as though Barry and Gary had sorted out the business. A stab of disappointment punctured my enthusiasm. I had been looking forward to a good punch-up. Since I had started working at Top Touch, I'd felt that I had to prove myself to the guys. It wasn't anything they said, or indicated in their attitude towards me. Perhaps it was because these guys were older and wiser than any other doormen that I had worked with, but I felt I needed to show them that I was on their level, and could handle anything that came up.

Later that night, I got my chance. My duster was securely fitted to my hand. That was a good job because, within a matter of seconds, some nutcase rushed out from the crowd and crashed straight into Chris, socking him in the side of his face. The guy was short, and I grabbed him. He bent low to ward off my blows, but I backed him against a pillar, and really gave it to him. Chris soon joined me, and while I was whacking him in the head, Chris was giving his stomach a good going over. The guy didn't stand a chance.

I began to enjoy myself. But suddenly, I felt a blow to my back. Turning round to see what was happening, I saw four or five guys backing Chris into the bar. They started to lay into him. Then I realized that I too was being set up. There were a couple of guys on either side of me. As I grabbed hold of them, we all toppled to the floor. Fortunately, I fell on top of them. I scrambled to my feet, and a missile of broken glass whizzed past my face, embedding itself in the wall. Heaving a sigh of relief, I turned and saw that virtually the whole nightclub had become a mass of fighting bodies. Chairs were being thrown everywhere. Glasses and bottles were flying through the air. I couldn't see Chris, or Barry or Gary.

Ian, I thought to myself, you have got to come out of this in one piece.

The guy who had launched the glass missile at me was still standing quite close by. I rugby-tackled him, and bundled him out through the fighting mass and through the double doors. He was trying to resist me, but he wasn't strong enough. At the top of the stairs, he started screaming; he knew what was coming. Showing no mercy, and loving every minute of it, I pitched him backwards down the stairs. He bounced and crashed his way to the bottom. Out of the corner of my eye, I saw the VIP lounge room being ransacked. The payphone was being pulled off the wall and someone was yanking the till off the bar. For a moment, I was at a loss as to what to do. Simon helped me make a decision.

'Quick, Ian! Barry's in trouble.'

I ran back through the doors, and saw that Barry had taken a bit of a beating. He was heaving himself up off the floor. His jacket had been ripped and blood was seeping from his face. A group of guys were still hovering around him, like wolves. They wanted more blood. I ran to Barry's aid. Then Gary came out of nowhere, and started to assess the situation.

'Right, that's it. It's over. Out! Everyone out.'

Taking a cue from him, I started to grab some of the troublemakers, herding them towards the door.

'Out, that's it, out.'

These guys were still resisting, but now there was a group of doormen ready to deal with more trouble, it was as though the wind had been taken out of their sails. At the top of the stairs, we shoved them hard. They soon got the message. Outside the club, as they spewed through the doors, I noticed some cops, sitting in their panda cars, passively looking on.

'Oi!' Chris shouted at them. 'You've been a great help, thanks!'

Back in the club it looked as if World War Three had taken place. The floor was a sea of broken glass. There wasn't a whole table or chair in sight. There were still about a hundred and fifty people in there, and amazingly the DJ still had the music belting out. This really wound Barry up. Making his way to the back of the club where the DJ had his spot, he yelled, 'Shut this music off. What's the matter with you? We've got to clear this place, and you still think it's party-time!'

The music stopped abruptly. We cleared the place, and then sat down to toast ourselves on a job well done.

We were really pleased with ourselves, even though some of us had taken a battering, were bloodstained and had ripped clothes.

The management finally came out from their hiding place – now that it was all over. They were satisfied with our efforts to quell the aggro, but I could tell that having their livelihood smashed up hadn't made them too happy.

Driving home, I was well pleased with myself. I felt that I had really proved something that night. Recounting in my mind the conversation that we had had after the fight, I felt smug and proud, as someone had noticed how I had thrown the guy down the stairs. It gave my ego a boost. I was glad that an opportunity had arisen for me to show these hard guys that I was up for it, and could handle myself. I was eager for another chance to prove myself.

◆   ◆   ◆

I had qualified for the British finals. I wanted 1989 to be a good year for me. If I won (which I was willing myself to do), it would be a step closer to getting a pro card, which would mean I could then compete professionally, and perhaps get sponsorship. It would also mean that I would at last be able to prove to Valerie that bodybuilding was indeed a viable occupation that had great benefits.

I continued to experiment with drugs. Now that I had crossed the line from drug-free to drug-filled, I was willing to put anything into my body, if it would help me to come first. I still listened to Sam about drugs; he knew a lot about them. He told me about a new 'wonder drug', which was injected straight into the bicep and immediately made the muscle swell. Sam gave me some, and I became a guinea pig.

As Sam held the ampoule to me, he taunted me. 'Do you really think you can do this?'

'Yes,' I replied, confidently. It wasn't hard for me to say. The desire to win was overwhelming. I did not want to lose ever again.

Most bodybuilders I knew were taking steroids, but what I was about to inject into my body was something that, at the time, nobody else was using. Back at home, I drew up the potion into the syringe, and injected it into my muscle. Instantly, before my eyes, my bicep increased in size. It was miraculous. Feeling very pleased with myself, I lay down on the settee and dozed off.

The doorbell rang. It was my older brother, Lloyd. He had come to see me, and to find out how my 'career' was progressing.

'C'mon then,' he said. 'Let's see your body.'

I was pleased that I had just injected myself, and that Lloyd would be the first to see the results. Lifting up my T-shirt, I preened myself in front of him. Smiling, he walked round me and said, 'Very nice, very nice.' Lifting my arms, I showed him my pumped-up biceps.

'What have you been doing?' he asked, shocked.

I was shocked myself. Since I had fallen asleep they had increased in size even more. I didn't want Lloyd to find out about my steroid-taking. Lloyd was very much against drugs, and he would have been disappointed if he had found out. Lying, I said to him, 'I've been doing a lot of cable curls.'

He started to reassure me that this was my year. He was certain I'd become British Champion.

4

KNOCK-BACK

Exhilarated – that's how I felt. The spotlights dazzled my eyes. The crowd was screaming and cheering. The MC for the evening was stirring the people up.

'C'mon,' he shouted, 'who's gonna win tonight?'

The crowd started yelling the names of their favourites. I heard my name. It was a boost to my already inflated ego. Air horns were tooting and music was blaring from the loudspeakers around the hall. Baby oil and sweat mingled together on my skin. My muscles stood out, glistening. I was centre-stage. In my heart I believed that I was already the winner. The trophy was right in front of me. I could almost feel the cool metal in my hands as I held the prize aloft to wild applause. My heart was beating rapidly. Clenching my fists, I wanted to jump up and down and shout, 'Yes, I've done it!' It was hard for me to contain myself.

The eyes of the judges continued to appraise each competitor. As the minutes ticked away, I was sure I was about to be announced as the winner.

'All right, folks,' boomed the MC. 'I have now been given the names of the winners.'

Everything went quiet.

'In sixth place . . .'

The MC called the names of the competitors, until he got to first. I was holding something in my hands. I wasn't sure what it was, or how it got there. I stood still, waiting.

'The 1989 British Bodybuilding Middleweight Champion is Ian . . . McCready.'

The noise that erupted in the arena was deafening. I was in shock. Ian McCready turned round and said to me, 'I thought you'd won.'

Numbness enveloped my brain. I couldn't think straight. Maybe our surnames had got mixed up and it should have been McDowall not McCready.

All the competitors, including me, were herded backstage. Only the winners of the first three places were left on stage to soak up the mighty applause from the audience.

Backstage, my brain kicked into gear. Looking down at my hands, I saw that I had been given a trophy.

'I can't believe you came fifth, Ian. Something's wrong,' said one of the guys who had been on stage with me.

'Yeah, man, you should've won,' everyone agreed.

I should really have been on that stage receiving all that acclaim. I looked at my trophy. It sickened me to see the word 'fifth'. In disgust I flung it on the floor, and walked off.

One of the competition officials came and offered me my expenses. Pushing him away, I said angrily, 'I don't want that. What do I want with that? You've robbed me.'

In the changing room, my mind somersaulted back to an incident that had occurred a month earlier. I had been doing a stint at the Bow gym. There weren't many people around, I was having a protein drink and Tony was sitting chatting to me. A sales rep came in and began to take stuff

out of his bag. He started giving us a sales spiel about his
bodybuilding products, and how good they were. He was
tall, skinny and bald. I started to take the mickey out of
him. I wanted to know how someone who looked like he
did could promote the benefits of such products.

'They haven't done anything for you, mate!' I said,
arrogantly.

Tony, by now, was in stitches. That only encouraged
me and I wouldn't let up. In the end, the guy packed up
and left, well upset.

A month later, during the morning of the championships, after the first round, I'd got changed and was
making my way across the arena with Sam, who was
telling me that I was the biggest and the best, and that I
was sure to win. Suddenly, a voice had bellowed out
behind me, 'Hey, boy!'

I didn't think whoever it was could be talking to me,
but nevertheless, I turned around. I was surprised to see
the skinny sales rep – in an official judge's blazer. What's
more, he had a badge saying that he was the head judge.

Pointing his finger at me he said, 'You were chewing
gum when you were on stage, weren't you?'

He was surrounded by some of the other judges. The
hairs on my arms stood up like soldiers to attention. I
sensed that this man was out to humiliate me. I assured
him that I hadn't been chewing gum. He looked me
straight in the eye. I could tell that he was loving every
minute of it; this was his moment of power. 'Yes, you
were. And for that, we have deducted five points from
your score.' He marched off.

I was upset and confused. Sam told me not to worry,
and that five points was nothing; it wouldn't make any
difference overall. I wasn't so sure.

Now that I had been placed fifth, I realized that the
judge had got his revenge. With this guy as the head

judge, I was never ever going to win an EFBB (English Federation of Body Builders) championship. I decided that the only thing to do was to change federations. I would now compete with the World Amateur Body Building Association (WABBA). There was no way that I was going to give up.

For months after my defeat, I couldn't get the fiasco out of my mind. My mood swung between rage, hatred and depression, but my determination did not falter. I wanted to be a winner.

At this time in my life nothing seemed to be going right. I trained and took more steroids, but they didn't help me to achieve a thing. I was consumed with myself. Valerie and my new daughter, Bianca, didn't get a look-in. Most of what I earned was spent on me. Valerie and I would have rows about money, and she was desperate for me to get a proper job. Normal employment was out of the question as far as I was concerned. I had made my mind up that I was going to continue with the body-building until I won, and nothing and no one was going to stop me. My wife said that she needed money for nappies and other baby paraphernalia. I loved my wife and child, but I loved 'me' more. I just couldn't part with much money. I needed it for *me*.

The arguments between Val and I were becoming more serious. We talked, or shouted, about going our separate ways, but living on my own again wasn't something I wanted to think seriously about. I didn't want to leave my baby girl. My dad had left me, and I didn't want Bianca to go through the same pain and rejection as I had. But at the same time, I had to do what I had to do.

We were living in a council flat on a big estate. My grey surroundings caused me to sink to lower depths of depression. I drove around in an old banger that repeatedly broke down. Nothing was working out for me. Why?

Someone had once told me that a curse had been put on my life. At the time, I thought this was rubbish. I didn't believe in witchcraft. It was all nonsense. Curses were only words, after all!

At 5 o'clock one morning, after walking in the rain for nearly an hour, I arrived home with my mood at rock bottom. My car had packed up again, and I didn't have the money to fix it or even get a cab home. Lying on my bed, exhausted, my thoughts came back to the curse. It seemed so irrational and stupid. But I had to admit, something was going on which I was powerless to change.

Money was one of my main problems. Like many people, I just didn't have enough.

I knew that my time at Top Touch would soon come to an end. Since the big fight, the club owners just couldn't pull it back again. The punters were becoming fewer and fewer, and we doormen were in danger of losing our jobs. I needed more work.

Then Al, one of the doormen at a club I used to do a few daytime stints at, asked if I could do him a really big favour.

''Ere, Ian, you busy tonight?'

'Why, what do you want?'

It was usual for the doormen to look after each other – just like family. He leaned towards me and whispered, 'Would you collect a shooter from Frank for me, and drop it up at Chimes tonight?'

'Yeah, yeah, no problem. I'll do it for you.'

Chimes was a nightclub in north London. It was really just a pub with a late licence, and well known for trouble. When I got to Frank's that evening, he told me that he wasn't too happy about giving Al the gun.

'You know what Al's like. He's a class one nutter. I don't want him killing anyone, and then have the shooter traced back to me.'

I nodded my head in agreement, but there wasn't much I could say or do. It was entirely up to Frank whether he let Al have the gun or not.

Outside Chimes that evening, I gave Al the nod. He quietly slipped away from his post and followed me to the car park. Opening the boot of my car, I pointed to the plastic bag concealing the gun. Al slipped it under his coat, and half-walked, half-ran back to the club, with me following. He went into the toilet to examine the piece while I had a look around the club. It was decorated nicely, as some nightclubs are. It wasn't as big as the Palais; it probably held 400 people max.

Al came out and said everything was all right, and thanked me for bringing him the gun. For the next half an hour, he whinged and moaned about working at Chimes. I listened with half an ear, but I knew that most of Al's problems were self-inflicted. Before I left, he offered me a shift. I took it because I needed the money.

A few weeks later I worked a Friday night at Chimes. What a night it was.

The earlier part of the evening was uneventful. The punters were out to have a good time and everything was quiet. There was just an hour or so left of the night when Beau, one of the other doormen, said that he had to use the loo. That left me at the front door, alone.

A group of guys approached the club, and asked to be let in. It was 1 o'clock and, as far as I was concerned, no one else was coming in.

'You're too late. The doors are shut,' I told them.

'What d'ya mean it's too late?' asked one of them, aggressively. 'Don't you know who I am?'

I shook my head. 'I don't care who you are. You're not coming in.'

I had been working as a doorman for a few years now and I was confident about my abilities. Facing a pack of

violent nutcases wasn't daunting; in fact, I thought of it
as a challenge. I mentally prepared myself to take them
on. I glanced over my shoulder to see if Beau was on his
way back. He wasn't, but no problem. Out of the corner
of my eye, I saw a group of punters approach me from
inside the club. One of them, shaggy hair trailing over
his face, towered over all of us.

'They're all right. They're with us. Just let 'em in,' he
said, gruffly.

Being surrounded by a sea of men who wanted to
cause trouble didn't intimidate me. I had grown so used
to violent encounters that it was just 'all in the line of
duty', as far as I was concerned.

While I was trying to reason with this guy, one of his
cronies had a go at me. His fist just caught the side of my
face. Instantly, I gave him a left hook. The big guy tried
to grab me in a bear hug, but I swung round quickly, and
uppercut him straight on his chin. He fell down in front
of me. The guy who had taken a swipe at me began to
back off. There was no way that I was going to let him
go, so I jumped on the head of the guy on the floor, and
ran out into the street. The guy I was after knew he
couldn't get away, so he stopped and curled himself up
into a ball. I began to pound him mercilessly. I was so
angry that he had dared to take a swing at me. All the
frustration and depression and every other negative
thing that had happened to me, I took out on this man.
He was my punch bag; I couldn't stop hitting him.

By now, the other doormen had been alerted to the
trouble.

Beau came up. 'C'mon, Ian, that's *enough*. Stop! That's
enough.'

I heard him, but I didn't want to stop. There was so
much pent-up anger inside me that needed to come out,
and I wanted to release it now. Eventually, Beau grabbed

me. It was a good thing he did, as the guy's face was a bloody pulp. As I had been hitting him with my bare hands, my knuckles were all busted-up and bloodied. I felt great.

The guy who had been aggressive, saying, 'Don't you know who I am?' was now up the road, being held back by his friends, shrieking, 'You don't know who you're messing with! I'm coming back for you.'

'Yeah?' I yelled back. 'Anytime!' Smiling, I walked back to the club.

The feud between these guys and us continued for a few weeks. I did a few more stints at Chimes, and they did come back. But we were waiting for them at the front door, so they drove off.

Al, who was the head doorman, had had enough at Chimes. He was offered a job running a pub.

"'Ere Ian, 'ow do you fancy my job?' he asked me one day.

It didn't take me long to make a decision. At Top Touch I was getting about £100 for the few shifts that I did each week. At Chimes, as head doorman, I would be working most nights. Also, I knew that whoever controlled the door controlled the moneybag, and I knew that I could have a little scam going to boost my earnings. So I said yes.

Within a fortnight of becoming the head doorman of Chimes, those guys came back to fulfil their threats. At the time, I was having a rare evening at home, relaxing with my family. A phone call from Beau put an end to that.

'Ian, you've got to come in. Wolfy and his mates have come back with reinforcements, and they're tooled up.'

'Who's Wolfy?' I asked.

'That guy who said he would be back for you. Did you know he stabbed some doorman at the Townhouse?'

'Why did you let them in?'

'We had to, we had no choice. There were loads of 'em.'

Sighing, I replaced the receiver. I could have done without this aggravation, but I knew the situation had to be dealt with. So I made a few phone calls and gathered some backup of my own. Then I headed for Chimes.

My car was full as I drove along the A406 towards north London. Jason was a young guy whose body filled up most of my car. I hadn't known him for long, so I gave him a pep talk.

'Listen, mate, here's my cosh.' I handed it to him with some reluctance. I didn't know if he could handle himself, and work as part of a team. 'Make sure you use it, right? I don't want to find that it's all gone off and you've kept this in your pocket.'

'No worries,' he assured me.

As I parked my car in front of the club, I could see fear and panic etched on the faces of Beau and Don. The car that was following me spewed its occupants onto the pavement, and we rushed for the door.

'The place has been cleared. Only the scum's left,' I was told. 'They know you're coming.'

'C'mon,' I said. 'Let's have 'em.'

Inside, there were about fifteen to twenty men gathered around the bar. As we pushed open the door, the men turned and watched as we approached them. I recognized the guy who had promised to come back and get me. Well, he'd kept his word. I knew that this situation had to be resolved. If it wasn't dealt with here and now, then that would be a signal for every nutcase in the area to come and try us out.

'Right,' I said, 'let's take this outside.' I didn't want the club to get smashed up.

Wolfy was a known local drug dealer. He obviously sampled his own wares, as his eyeballs were popping out of his head. In fact, most of his crew looked well tanked-up. I knew this could prove to be deadly.

Taking deep breaths of night air, my mind focused on the job.

Don pointed his finger in Wolfy's face. 'Now, listen, you . . .'

Unfortunately Don wasn't very streetwise. If he had been, he would have known to hit first and talk later. Wolfy whacked him. Dazed, Don staggered, clutching his face. I couldn't see if Wolfy had a tool in his hand or not, but I wasn't taking any chances. I smashed him in the eye with my new spiky knuckle-duster. His head shot back. But before I had time to follow that punch with another, he retaliated and caught me on the nose. He was like a crazed animal. Profanities spewed out of his mouth.

My mind was whirling. I had to take this guy out quick. He was proving to be more of a problem than I had expected. I hit him three or four times. Finally, he collapsed in a heap.

Turning the knuckle-duster round to the stabbing implement, I plunged it a few times into the leather jacket he was wearing and gave him a few good kicks to his head. He didn't move.

Looking over my shoulder, I saw that the whole place was in uproar. Jason had taken my advice. He was wielding the cosh like a professional. Some of Wolfy's cronies could see that they didn't have a chance against us, so they ran off.

Back in the club, we were pleased at how it had all gone. The manager was pale and looked frightened, even though he had been holed up in the back of the club during the action.

'I've called the police. They'll be here any minute,' he informed us.

What a fool! I wanted to yell at him. That's the last thing you do! I was just about to tell the guys to get rid of their tools when there was a banging at the door. Looking through the glass, I could see it was Wolfy, covered in blood and gore. He looked like an extra from a horror movie. Screaming like a demented devil, he roared, 'Open up! I'm gonna have you.' I was exasperated. Was this man indestructible?

I pushed the door open, catching Wolfy unawares. He stumbled backwards. Straightening up, he stood facing us with a big blade in his hand.

'C'mon, then. Who's first?'

Before I could think of what to do next, one of the other guys threw some liquid over him. He immediately clutched his face and shrieked in agony. I could tell by the smell that he had been doused with ammonia. We quickly closed the doors.

It wasn't long before bricks and stones, and any other missile they could get their hands on, came crashing through the window. My boys wanted to go outside and finish them off. I told them no. Our business now was to hide our weapons, and wait for the police. They came and arrested the troublemakers. All in all, it was a good night's work.

I knew that news of this 'war' would spread around north London like wildfire. I was glad, because that meant that other troublemakers would keep away.

Being head doorman was good for me. My self-esteem increased and I felt more positive about myself. The large quantity of steroids that I was consuming made me feel like Superman. The depression was held at bay when I was working and when I trained, although it would seep back into my life outside of those times. My goal was still intact – winning. And this time I was going to do it.

5

DARK AND LIGHT

The day was bright and sunny. Walking along the road I felt good – free, without a care in the world.

In an instant, the day was engulfed by blackness. Everywhere and everything was covered in darkness. 'What's happening?' I cried. I was alone, and fear gripped my heart like a vice.

The black sky cracked open and a brilliant shaft of light beamed into the darkness, swallowing it up whole. The light was blinding and I was dazed and confused. The light was powerful. I fell down on my face – the light had a strength that I couldn't fight. I lay prostrate, unable to move.

Is this the end for me?

'Ian, Ian, wake up! What's wrong?'

My heart was beating as though I had just run 100 miles, and I was drenched in sweat. I climbed out of bed and made my way to the kitchen. Valerie was behind me, still asking what was wrong.

'Nothing,' I said.

'Well it must've been *something*. Look at the state you're in.'

'Nah, nah.' I shook my head. The frightening dreams that I had been having were not something that I wanted to share with Val right now. They were freaking me out. I tried to work out why this was happening to me. When I was awake, my life seemed filled with aggravation. Nothing was going right. I had to fight to get everything. And now I was being robbed of sleep because of these nightmares. I had never suffered from bad dreams before; why now? I racked my brain to think of someone I could talk to about them. The only person I could think of was a psychiatrist, but they would probably want to lock me up. So I tried to work out what was going on in my brain myself.

The daytime had its own worries. Through my excessive steroid consumption, I had developed gynaecomastia. Fat deposits had formed hard lumps behind my nipples, and they had increased in size. The pain was excruciating. My fear was that I would end up with full-blown gynaecomastia, and that my chances of competing in Japan would go out of the window. Allan had promised that he would get me some pills which were supposed to reverse the side-effects of the drugs that had caused the problem in the first place. Each time I visited the gym, he told me, 'I'll get them tomorrow.' But tomorrow never seemed to come. Many bodybuilders took the drug to combat the side-effects of the steroids, but I could never lay my hands on it.

I had only two weeks left in which to get the matter cleared up. I was desperate.

My friend Sam advised me to come off the steroids completely.

'No way. I'm going to compete and win, and go on to Japan.' My determination was as strong as ever.

A week before the competition, Allan turned up with a few hundred tablets. I scoffed them down like a pig. I assumed that by taking a large number of them, they would work more quickly to reverse the problem. But there was no change at all. I was furious.

'What are these tablets, chalk?' I was disgusted. After all this time, my condition was the same. The irony was that my body had never been in such tiptop shape as it was now – 14 stone of pure muscle. I looked good; a winner. I knew that I was by far the best I had ever been. I decided to go for it.

The South East Championships were being held in Basildon. I had been dieting for a whole year. My diaries detailed every gram of food that I had eaten. I kept a record of every workout. The steroids that I had taken were logged. I was very serious about bodybuilding: it was my life; it was at the centre of my being. I was going to get through. My devotion paid off. I qualified for the finals in Japan.

Backstage, one of the organizers of the competition called me aside.

'Listen, Ian, you were fantastic. I have no doubt that you'll do well in Japan, but you have got to get that gynaecomastia sorted.'

I nodded. 'I don't know what to do. I've been taking medication, but it hasn't worked.'

'Look, take this number, and give this guy a call. He'll sort you out.'

I looked down at the piece of paper that he had given me. I knew the name of the guy. 'Yeah, I'll give him a call.'

Ricardo owned a small gym in Stratford. He had been the World Bodybuilding Champion a number of years ago. He was a well-respected man, and so I took his advice.

'I'll make arrangements for you to be operated on. Don't worry, you won't miss Japan,' he promised. 'It'll probably cost you about £500. Is that a problem?'

Shaking my head, I told him no. I was so pleased that at last I was getting the gynaecomastia treated. If he had told me it was going to cost me a million pounds, some-how, somewhere, I would have found the cash. But unfortunately for me, it all fell through. I never did find out why; all I knew was that I was back to square one. Ricardo was embarrassed that despite all his careful planning I was still stuck.

'I'll tell you what, Ian, let's take a drive down to the Roding Hospital, and see what they can do for you.'

I was willing to try anything.

The Roding Hospital was a private establishment. They informed me that the operation, which could be carried out within the month, would set me back £1,500. I booked myself in. Now I just had to get the money. It shouldn't be too difficult; I would just have to steal more money from the club. As people paid to get in, I would stuff a few notes into my pocket. Whereas before, I worked out the money on a ratio of two for the club and one for me, it would now be one for the club and two for me. It would only be for a few weeks, and I wasn't going to let anything stand in the way of my operation. In my drug peddling, it would be easy for me to rip people off. I didn't care about anyone. My number one priority was me.

It wasn't long before I got the money together. Japan, here I come, I thought. But the Friday night before the Monday when I was due to have the operation was a liv-ing nightmare that would have far-reaching conse-quences.

A young woman ran to the front door. 'Quick! There's a fight.' Don and I charged into the club, and made our way to where the trouble was. Two young guys were going at each other hammer and tongs.

'C'mon now, break it up, break it up.'

I grabbed one guy, Don grabbed the other. As I was restraining the guy, someone shouted to me, 'Look, he's got "squirt"!'

Looking down, I saw he had a plastic bottle of nasal spray – I knew it was ammonia. This was a substance that was easy to obtain. I tore the bottle out of his hand and, grabbing him by the scruff of his neck, ran him through the exit door, which sprung open as the guy's head made contact with it. He flew down the steps and landed on the ground.

'You're barred, and don't come back!' I yelled after him.

I had wanted to get rid of this guy for weeks, and now I had the perfect opportunity. Shutting the door, I felt pleased that at last I had seen the back of a menace. Later that evening, although I didn't see him, I saw his handiwork.

I was standing inside the club. Suddenly, there was a loud banging on the front door. Through the square window, I saw a frantic young woman.

'There's some madman smashing up a car in the car park with an axe!'

The car park couldn't be seen from the front of the building. Opening the door, I charged out towards the car park. The other doormen were right behind me. A thought entered my head. Could it be my car? A surge of hatred welled up inside me.

As soon as I saw my car, I roared, 'Where is he? I'm gonna kill 'im!' I ran to the end of the car park. A high brick wall enclosed it, and I knew that this guy wasn't hiding behind it. He, very wisely, had disappeared. I ran back to my car. All the windows were smashed. The axe marks were deeply imprinted in the door panels. Profanities were flying through the air as the other doormen expressed their outrage.

Then Beau said, 'I think I know where he lives. Don't worry, we'll get him.'

Rage boiled over and gushed out of me. I wanted blood. I began to furiously kick at the big tree nearby.

My mood was murderous. I couldn't contain myself; I demanded that Beau find out for me *now* where the guy lived. And a posse of about thirty of us, including doormen from other clubs, drove to the alleged address.

The large sprawling housing estate was dimly lit. As carload after carload pulled up, people began to peep out of their windows. We found the flat that the guy was supposed to live in. Kicking the door in, we stormed into the flat, going from room to room. Each room was practically a shell. The only inhabitants were junkies, stoned out of their heads. Fear showed in their empty eyes. A young girl started to scream. I began to ask where this guy was, but the junkies denied that he lived there.

'Right! The next time you see 'im, tell 'im he's dead.' I meant it.

That night I got a lift home. Reluctantly, I made my way to my flat; I didn't want to go home. Sleep would be a long time coming. I didn't want to rest until I had dealt with the guy. My mind kept replaying the state of my car. My car! How was I going to function from day to day without it? My anger dissipated and depression came to the fore. A heaviness descended on me. My mind became fogged; thinking was an effort. My life is cursed, I thought to myself. Things were just going from bad to worse. How could things go so dramatically wrong, and at this crucial time?

I retrieved the car the next day. Driving through the traffic was embarrassing. Every eye was on me. People in the street stood and pointed. I was hoping that the police wouldn't pull me up.

The mechanic who was going to repair my car told me that it would cost in the region of £300. Shrugging, I said, 'Whatever.' I had the money put away for the operation, but I felt that somehow I could lay my hands on more before Monday. That was, until I got home. I had been sent a letter from the hospital, with an itemized bill for the operation. What they hadn't told me at the time of giving me an estimate was that the anaesthetist's charges had not been included. Altogether, I would now owe another £800. Shaking my head, I let defeat jump all over me. Throughout my life, I had done everything possible to achieve my goals, but now it seemed to me that something was definitely working against me. The trouble was I couldn't see what was causing me this grief. My heart sunk lower – no Japan. My guts wrenched and twisted as I agonized over my lost opportunity.

. . . The light was powerful. I fell down on my face – the light had a strength that I couldn't fight. I lay prostrate, unable to move. My very thoughts were exposed to the light – I was completely naked under its bright glare. Surely it was time for me to die?

I couldn't stay in bed. Life was getting so that I didn't want to be awake in the day, and I didn't want to go to sleep at night. I'd had this nightmare about four times. It was always the same. I didn't want to tell Valerie about this. I didn't want her to think that I was weak, and couldn't handle a few scary dreams. The problem was, I didn't have anyone I could talk to about them. If I had tried to share my dream experiences with any of the doormen, they would have thought I had gone mad.

I sat alone, in the dark, in the front room, troubled. The thought did occur to me that perhaps I had gone off my head and all the bashes I had taken to my skull had now resulted in me losing my mind. Then a memory of a conversation I'd had with my friend Marcus, Valerie's brother, came back to me very clearly. We were 13 years old. It was a cold, wet night, and we were sitting in a dark alleyway, sniffing glue. We started to talk about heaven and hell.

'I believe in heaven and hell. And you need to know Jesus to get to heaven,' Marcus had said, with a confidence that I put down to the glue. I was shocked and upset that Marcus was telling me, in a roundabout way, that I wouldn't be going to heaven, because I didn't know Jesus.

'You what? What's Jesus got to do with it? Look, if you're good, you're going to heaven, if there is such a place, and if you're bad, you're going to hell, if there is such a place.' I hadn't been too sure about what I was saying, but it had made sense to me.

'Listen here,' Marcus had arrogantly replied. 'God has set a standard. Everybody, no matter how good they are, has fallen short of God's standard. Everyone at some point in their life has stolen, lied, thought bad thoughts about someone, or done worse. And everyone, whether they believe in Jesus or not, is going to be held accountable for everything that they have ever said or done. Jesus, God's only son, when he was on this earth, was the only man ever to have lived who didn't do a wrong thing. Only believing in him, and receiving him as the Lord of your life, will save you from going to hell.'

'Don't talk rubbish!' I'd shouted, fuming. 'You're telling me my mum is going to hell? What kind of a God lets innocent people suffer? My mum hasn't done anything wrong!'

Marcus had said, mockingly, 'Get a life, Ian. Not only has your mum done wrong, but so have you. And,' he'd continued, 'so has the whole world.'

I'd wanted to punch his lights out for talking about my mum like that. I'd got up and walked away from him, glancing over my shoulder and thinking, who does he think he is? He's got a bag of glue in his hand, sitting there talking like a hypocrite.

In the darkness of the front room, a ray of light beamed into my mind: Marcus. That was the person who might understand what I was going through. I couldn't sleep, so I sat and waited until the first light of day, and then I called him.

What he told me wasn't what I wanted to hear. Boldly, Marcus said, 'Ian, Jesus is calling you. He is the light . . .'

I didn't give him a chance to go on. I said, 'Look, Marcus, I don't want to hear all that. I just want the dreams to stop. I've got enough problems in my life. I haven't got time to get religious.'

'OK, mate, I hear you,' he replied. 'But if you have another dream, call out to Jesus and ask him into your life. Believe me, after that your dreams will stop.'

'I don't know about Jesus coming into my life, but I *definitely* want the dreams to stop.'

The conversation that I had with Marcus didn't make me feel any better. I tried to think of someone else who might be able to help me. My wife? But as she was Marcus's sister and had had the same kind of upbringing, I knew it would be a waste of time telling her. My wife went to church periodically. We had reached an agreement years before that I wouldn't talk about violence and she wouldn't discuss God. I wanted to keep to that.

A few nights later I had another dream – with a variation at the end.

. . . I fell down on my face – the light had a strength that I couldn't fight. I lay prostrate, unable to move. Suddenly, I was standing up. My feet moved as I walked in the direction of a city. The bright light was behind me, following where I was going. Approaching the city, I first saw people going about

*their business. On closer inspection, I saw that the people did-
n't have any eyes. Fear gripped me; I didn't want to go further.
But something evil, like a force, was pulling me closer and
closer to the city. I tried to resist, but the evil force was
stronger than me. I heard a warm, loving voice behind me, yet
at the same time inside me, say, 'This is where you're going,
Ian, unless you call on me.'*

I woke up. Petrified, and shaken by the dream, I woke
Valerie up. I no longer cared how I looked to her. I needed help. I could no longer hold back the tears.

'Val, I've had a terrible dream.'

Sleepily, she asked me about it. When I had finished
she said, 'Ian, let's pray and ask Jesus to take away these
dreams, and ask him to come into your life.'

'C'mon, let's do it now,' I replied desperately. At that
point, I would have done anything to be free of those
nightmares. The funny thing was, after we had prayed I
felt peaceful. Calmness settled on me which replaced the
fear. I slept like a baby.

For the next few days, I kept wondering if that short
prayer that I had prayed with my wife could really make
me into a Christian. I wasn't . . . surely? Looking in the
mirror, I appeared to be the same. And deep down, my
emotions and attitudes were the same. Yet, every now
and again I would think about God. Could he be real?
Who was Jesus? What did it mean that he was the Son of
God? Mental pictures of him on the cross would seep
into my mind, and I would stop what I was doing to
ponder upon them. We had been given a Bible as a wedding present. I tried to read it, but it didn't seem to make
much sense, although the stories about Jesus were inter-
esting.

Depression still hung around my neck like a noose.
My dream of becoming World Champion seemed to be

so far out of my reach. The gynaecomastia was still a problem, and raising the money for the operation was proving to be difficult.

My job at Chimes was becoming very violent. Every night I was fighting and beating people up. I enjoyed every punch and kick, and whatever else I could do to inflict harm upon someone. One night, the violence escalated out of control. This particular night, it erupted into a mini war.

The police came and arrested all the doormen, including me. I spent a miserable weekend banged up in a police cell. They questioned me relentlessly about the incident. At one point, in the break from being interviewed by the police, I laid on the bed, after counting all the specks on the cell's ceiling, and walking up and down. I wondered why, even after praying that prayer with Valerie, my life seemed to be out of control. Since that prayer, I had tried to be good. Yet I had gone in completely the opposite direction and was even worse than I had been before. My mind was jumping all over the place. I reasoned that if God knew everything, and he knew that I was trying hard to get on the right side of him, why had I ended up in this predicament? Why had he let my life go so wrong? Did he really have the power to help me? All the training I had done in the last five or six years was for nothing. I had not been able to go on to compete in a major competition. Where was God in all of that?

The outcome of my arrest was that I was charged with violence and disorder. It carried a five-year-plus imprisonment, if found guilty. But having this charge hanging over my head didn't deter me from my violent behaviour. A couple of months later, I was embroiled in more brutal activities. Another big fight broke out in Chimes. We doormen steamed in, grabbed bodies and threw them out of the exit door. Nearly everyone got a slap or punch to help them on their way. Twenty minutes later, a loud bang was heard outside. We rushed out of the door and round to the side of the building.

One of the guys we had thrown out had made a Molotov cocktail and had pitched it against the side of the club. It hadn't exploded but he had another ready in his hand. He threw it towards the club. I didn't wait to see what would happen, I just charged at him.

'What do you think you're doing?' I yelled.

'Nothing,' he replied, cockily.

He was over six foot tall. I glanced behind him, and saw that his mates were filling up more bottles from the petrol station.

'Nothing?' I punched him straight on his jaw. He fell backwards and crashed to the ground, so I kicked him a few times. One of the doormen punched him while he was down. The guy was now unconscious. John, another doorman, was beating a guy with his cosh.

I shouted to all the doormen, 'Let's get back inside, before the Old Bill come.' With a few last kicks and punches, we retreated back into the club. We had a few drinks, and a joke about the fight.

'Ian, you knocked that geezer out with one punch. You are bad, man,' laughed one of the doormen. I felt proud hearing the comments from the guys. The fact that they had seen me in action, looking good, made me feel a bit better about myself.

Driving home alone, I replayed the fight again in my mind. Proud and boastful feelings were suddenly replaced with guilt. This was a feeling that I had rarely, if ever, experienced before, particularly in association with my work. I began to argue with myself. The geezer deserved what I gave him, he was taking liberties. But another thought entered my head. You shouldn't have hit him. Pangs of guilt flashed through my mind and it was hard to shift them. I was just doing my job, I reasoned with myself.

I pulled over into a lay-by on the A406. I had to take hold of my mind, something I couldn't do while I was driving. I needed to think about these new thoughts.

As I was sitting alone in the car, a voice, although inaudible, was speaking into me: 'You've done something wrong.' I kept reasoning, arguing and wrestling with myself about the incident. Then, other situations came into my mind. And slowly, like the breaking of day, I began to realize that I truly had done wrong. In fact, all of my life I had been living by the wrong values. What Marcus had told me was true. I could feel the essence of the truth deep inside of me. No one had to tell me, 'Ian, you're wrong.' For the first time in my life, I now grasped the fact that I was in the wrong. That truth hit me like a sledgehammer. Not only was the violence wrong, but everything I was doing was wrong. I don't know how I knew, but believe me, I knew! I thought about the times I had used the name of Jesus as a swear word, and I literally cringed. The shame of what I had said covered me. I felt very unclean – dirty. From childhood, I had been surrounded by people swearing and behaving in a questionable manner, and it had never worried me, until now.

Leaning back against the seat, I felt terrible. Never had anyone or anything invoked such emotions in me, causing me to become aware of myself. I cried out: 'Jesus, if you're real, help me, change me, take away this filth from my life. Forgive me, Jesus.'

A tingle erupted over my body. What was happening to me? I could feel warmth slowly entering my stony heart, and the power of it cracked it open. The thick darkness and evil that had dominated my heart seemed to seep out as this other power, which I can only describe as a strong love, filled me up. After a while, I felt clean. It was like when a torrent of rain cascades down, and then after it has passed everywhere looks bright and clean. That was me. Clean. Tears streamed down my face; I couldn't control myself: I was weeping like a baby. The strange thing was, I assumed at the time that it was me just coming to an understanding of the reality of how I had been living and that I could now see things differently. It happened so naturally, without human intervention, that it was hard to imagine that it was all down to Jesus. In a matter of an hour or so, I had come to know that Jesus was real; he was alive. What I had experienced wasn't a figment of my imagination, I had actually gone through something. Jesus was spiritually tangible to me. Before, I didn't even know that I possessed a spirit. Now, I was sure that I had one.

Truly, as I drove off, I knew that that experience in the lay-by had changed me – forever. I was a new Ian McDowall.

6

PEACE AND TURMOIL

Sitting in church a few Sundays after my conversion, I felt like a fish out of water. Everyone around me looked content and settled in themselves. I did feel very peaceful – the most peaceful I have ever felt, in fact. But, something was missing. No more did I sleep with a knife under my pillow, with one eye open ready to defend myself if need be; I could sleep the night through. I was feeling a whole lot cleaner inside, but not totally comfortable.

I was handed the collection bag and I dropped some money into it. Then it dawned on me – the money that I had just given was not clean. I might have a cleaned-up heart and life that was forgiven by God, but there were areas of my life that were still shrouded in the darkness of sin. I was still nicking money from the door at Chimes. Shame welled up inside me. I glanced around and felt that people knew I was a fraud and a thief.

Blocking these awful thoughts from my mind, I tried to listen to what the pastor was preaching: 'God commands many things that he expects us to live by. For example, he tells us not to commit adultery for the preservation of family life. Again, God tells us not to steal; we should be satisfied with what he has provided for us. God expects us, especially fathers and husbands, to work honestly to provide for our families.'

Those words burnt into my soul. I could feel the heat of the truth seeping deep into my heart. To be truthful, I could've got up and walked out. But I stayed, listening to his words as they hammered into my conscience. I tried to switch off his voice. It was difficult. I began to wrestle with what he was saying and the lifestyle that I wanted to hang on to.

'How can I live without money?'

'. . . Trusting God, giving your life to him, enables you to live without the fear of not having food, clothes, and paying bills. God's mighty power provides for us. Ask any Christian and they will tell you it's true.'

'The steroids cost loads of money. This guy doesn't understand,' I reasoned to myself.

By the time church was over, I was hot and flustered. I wanted to get away and be by myself to think. I couldn't share this with Valerie because this is exactly what she had been telling me again and again. But I was determined to win the World Championships, and there was no way I could stop now.

The next morning I was back in the gym. It amazed me that although I was changing inside, outside everything looked the same. I threw myself into lifting weights. My body was there, but my mind wasn't. The pastor's voice was like a non-stop recording in my head. I knew I had to change the way I was living, the way I was getting money, but how? And, more importantly, how could I get hold of enough money legally to keep me, Val and our baby? Could Jesus really provide for me? How did you trust God?

I wished I could just take my mind out of my body and lay it down for a while. I was so much in my head I thought I was going crazy. Yet, when I prayed – talked to God about my situation – I would feel peaceful. It was odd; I didn't have to deal with these issues before I became a Christian, so why was I dealing with them now? I couldn't explain it to anyone, so I kept it to myself.

Working at Chimes nightclub was strictly to earn money. The first few months after I gave my life to Christ, I still felt comfortable with the familiar surroundings. But each night as I drove to work, I could sense a shifting of my feelings; a battle was taking place in my mind as to whether I should be doing the job or not.

People around me commented on the change they felt and saw in me. The other doormen I worked with would tell me: 'Ian, mate, something's different about you . . . you've stopped swearing, or have you had a haircut or something?'

I would laugh and make some wisecrack. I couldn't bring myself, yet, to tell them what had happened to me. How could I? I was taking backhanders, and steroids – how could I say I was a Christian? I was a number one hypocrite!

Des was one of the doormen that I was really friendly with, although I couldn't even tell him about my changed life. 'Hey, Ian,' he said one day. 'I've got a proposition for you.'

I was all ears in case I could earn myself some more dosh. He bent close to my ear and whispered, 'There's a right tasty bird that's been after you for weeks. She's asked me to put in a good word for her, so I am. What do you reckon?'

My heart thumped and my mouth was dry. I knew who he meant. I had already clocked her and he was right – she was quite a tasty bit of stuff. But guilt kicked in straight away and I began to shake my head.

'Oi, what's up, mate? Are you trying to tell me you're not interested? Leave it out! Next you'll be telling me you're going to join a monastery.'

I laughed. What an ironic statement. Des didn't know how close he was to the truth.

I loved Valerie and had never cheated on her; sleeping with a woman other than my wife was totally out of the question. But when this woman – through Des – offered herself to me on a plate, just for a nanosecond a hint of temptation was there. I thought it strange that before I was a Christian I didn't struggle with adulterous ideas, yet that night I had to keep pushing the thought out of my mind. It was as though 'someone' was purposely putting the temptation into my head. But I wasn't taking it any further, and I knew for sure that God had restrained me so I was able to say no and really mean it.

The money issue was still there, though. Each night I would have a fair amount of dough in my pockets. I would count it out, and once all the bills had been taken care of the rest was for my own personal use. I was reading my Bible every day without fail, never missed church, and I knew my heart, mind and attitude to life was changing. But still I couldn't let go of the money – and anger was still a problem. Since I had become a Christian, I was proud that I had kept my anger under control and I hadn't been in one fight. That was soon to change.

My shift started off peacefully. All the punters paid and stepped into the club, no hassle. Then a guy came up to me, reeking of alcohol. He was swaying a bit, full of abuse and bad language.

'Let me in, here's my money.' He pushed his shoulder into me. I let that go.

'No, mate, sorry,' I told him. 'Go home and sort yourself out.'

His mouth was like a sewer. He ranted and raved, cursed and swore. I reined myself in and reasoned that he was out of his head. Each time I opened the door, he tried to get in, but I stopped him.

Then, as I opened the door to let someone out, the guy became irate. He spat what seemed like a huge amount of spittle into my face. Instantly, not stopping to think about turning the other cheek, I punched him solidly in the face and he fell to the ground. I bent over to give him some more, when he grabbed my arm. For a split second I wanted to hurt him. Then, unclenching my fists, I straightened up, and some of the other doormen dragged me into the club.

Looking through the window at the man trying to get up off the ground with blood streaming down his face, I experienced a new feeling – forgiveness! I knew that Jesus had forgiven me for my scumbag life, and now I could extend that feeling and forgive this guy. I felt sorry for him. Here he was, drunk, broken, his face smashed in, no hope in his life, thinking that getting into the club was going to be good for him, and I had damaged him. I wanted to go outside and tell him that he needed Jesus, that he should give his life to God. But how could I? It seem impossible to tell him that Christ loved him and had died for him, when I had just probably broken his nose, or at least damaged his self-esteem. Would he take any notice of me? Plus, the guys around me would think I was mad.

My Christian life up until this point was a constant struggle – knowing what I should do that was right and good, and yet not doing it. One morning I was reading my Bible and I was shocked to see this same conflict was mentioned in the book of Romans, chapter 7.

I was still reluctant to tell my mates what had happened to me. It was beginning to weigh me down. Then, in the gym one afternoon, I was put on the spot. The guy who owned the gym, Ricardo, had a brother called Xavier. Xavier had just become a Christian, and he was full of it. He couldn't stop talking about Jesus, and the guys were listening, and laughing at him. I hung back. I couldn't join in with the guys; I knew what Xavier was saying was true.

Valerie was with me that day, doing some weights. Without missing a beat she piped up, 'Ian's become a Christian, haven't you, Ian?'

All eyes were on me. I felt myself blush a deep red, and hung my head, mumbling rubbish. I still couldn't bring myself to admit that Xavier was right. My heart was thumping. I wanted to say something, but I couldn't. Later, Valerie asked me why I didn't speak up. Again, I just mumbled something that didn't make sense. I felt bad that I had hidden my faith in Christ.

I prayed that I would get another chance to tell people about my faith, and it came in an unexpected way.

Esmond, Es for short, was a doorman and a great friend of mine. He was black, six foot four, and no one messed around with him. We had a lot of laughs together, and we fought alongside each other. One day, Es told me he was having trouble with a doorman at the Ilford Palais nightclub.

'What do you reckon, Ian? Come with me to sort the geezer out?'

I was happy to help him; Es was a good mate. It was midweek, and even though I knew the club was busy, it wouldn't be packed. Once inside we took the stairs up to the first floor. Es was just ahead of me and a few other guys that had come along for some action. We stopped in the foyer as eight bouncers in suits and bow ties eyed us.

Es launched into one of the bouncers, accusing him of troubling one of his mates. The guy denied it.

'Do you know what? You're a liar,' sneered Es. 'And you know what happens to liars.'

Es swung a punch at the guy, who instantly fell down. Another guy grabbed Es round the throat and began to throttle him. I jumped in and gripped that guy round the neck. A huge guy came alongside me; his trench coat flapped open and I saw a pickaxe under his arm.

Me, Es and the guy whose arm was round his throat were locked together. Out of the corner of my eye, I glimpsed another guy with a washing-up liquid bottle in his hand. He squirted the contents over us. The liquid blinded me. The smell and the awful burning sensation told me all I needed to know. Ammonia!

Falling to the floor, I couldn't breathe. I was scared that I had been blinded for life. My lungs were having difficulty drawing in oxygen – this is it, I thought. I couldn't even think about God at this moment in time; all I wanted was to be able to see and breathe.

An ambulance came and took us to the hospital. After being checked over, eyes rinsed out, mouth and lungs given the all-clear, I was sent home. But Es had to be operated on. The guy with the pickaxe had struck a blow to my mate's head, damaging his eye socket and splitting open his jaw. He had to have metal plates in his face.

Days after this altercation I wondered how it could have happened. I was supposed to be a Christian now; how had I got into this fight? From the outset, I should have tried to talk Es and the other guys out of it. I should have prayed. I should have been the peaceful bystander who tried to negotiate a non-violent outcome. Instead, I had been up the front, urging the fight on, willing to get involved, doing what I had to do to help my friend. I didn't foresee the end result. What was God telling me?

For a few weeks I kept a low profile. Apparently, the police had been asking questions – no way did I want to be linked with this.

I hadn't seen Es since he had come out of hospital, and eventually decided the time was right to go and visit him. Stepping into his front room, I was shocked at his appearance. His head was swollen to twice its normal size, his eye had dropped and there was a split from his lower lip to his chin; even his teeth were cracked open. The curtains were drawn; it was dark except for a small lamp on a side table that gave off a dim light.

'What's happening, mate?' I didn't know what else to say.

Slowly shaking his head he whispered, 'I can't take this, man. Look at me.' He began to cry.

I didn't want to, but I forced myself to look at him.

'I can't stand up, I get dizzy. I can't see out this eye. I can't eat, I can't swallow, I can't sleep.' Glancing up he went on, 'I can't live like this, Ian. If I go out, anyone could take liberties and I couldn't do nothing.'

I couldn't help him physically. It seemed as though the doctors had done all they could. What could I tell him? Clearing my throat, I gave him the only bit of news I could. 'Es, you need Jesus.'

He looked at me as if I was strange. I carried on. 'Jesus can definitely heal you. He can set you free.'

There, I'd said it. Es was the first person I had told about Jesus.

'Ian, look at me.' He held out his arms. 'Don't you think I've got enough to sort out in my life? I don't need no more problems, mate.'

I couldn't keep quiet. 'A few months ago I gave my life to Jesus,' I began. Holding nothing back, I told Es what had happened to me and how I was still going through changes on the inside. He listened, shrugged a few times, and that was it.

Driving home, I started to panic. Did Es think I was nuts? Had I made a fool of myself? Would he now tell the whole world that I was a Christian, and would that stop me getting work? Should I have still kept it to myself? All these negative thoughts and more were churning around my brain.

Saturday, only a few days after I had been to see him, he turned up with a mate at Chimes to see me.

'Ian, you've got to help me,' he said. 'Either I top myself – or Jesus has got to heal me, like you said he would.'

7

THE POWER OF GOD

The Canning Town church in east London was kicking. Walking through the school doors where the church was held every Sunday, my expectation for God to intervene in Es's life was high. I knew that Es's only hope was Jesus; not only for his healing, but for a change of heart too. This was what I was slowly beginning to realize – it was not the external things of a person's life that necessarily needed to change; it was the *emotions and thoughts* that needed to be transformed, to bring about the peace and happiness that most people seemed to lack . . . me included.

I wanted Es to be prayed for, but this particular Sunday it was not to be. Taking Es home, I asked him how he was doing.

'I still hurt like hell, mate, but you know what? I felt sort of peaceful in that place.'

I knew what he meant. This peace was something precious, and unless they experienced it, other people didn't have a clue what you were talking about.

Marcus had invited Es to a midweek meeting at Kensington Temple in west London. I couldn't make it as I was working, but I was well pleased that Marcus was now involved with Es and it wasn't just me that was 'carrying' him on my own.

Later that night, about 3 a.m., Es called me. I was exhausted, and at first I couldn't make out what he was going on about.

'Ian, Ian, Jesus has healed me!'

'What?'

The gist of it was that yes, he was now healed. I told him that I would check him out tomorrow. So, early the next day, I found myself seated across the table from Es, who was heartily tucking into his breakfast.

'Food never tasted so good, mate,' he grinned.

I was astounded by Es's appearance. His eye no longer drooped. The hole in his chin and teeth was closed, as though there had never been an injury there in the first place. His mouth was crammed with bacon and eggs and he was still shovelling more into it.

'Jesus is real!' Es said between mouthfuls.

'What happened, then?' I asked.

Smiling as he slurped down some tea, Es began to tell me how he got miraculously healed.

'Right, then.' He wiped his mouth. 'On the train to the church, Marcus kept going on about the need for me to forgive anyone who had done anything to me. In my mind I thought, no way. Once I was up and running again I was making it my business to hunt down this guy and deal with him, kill him if I had to. The man had tried to *kill* me. I couldn't let someone get away with that.

Walking into Kensington Temple, I looked up and told God that I would forgive the guy that had done this to me. In fact, all the people in my life that had messed me up, I would forgive them too. Marcus and I sat at the back of church and listened to the guy. When the service was nearly over, the guy said something like, "You at the

back, stand up." Everyone was looking around and
Marcus said to me, "He means you, mate."

'I didn't want to stand up, but I did. Everyone was
looking at me. This guy, I think his name was Charles
Slagle, began to tell me about my life. I looked down at
Marcus, and I was a bit annoyed because I thought that
he had been mouthing off about me to this guy. Then he
said to me: "Thank you for forgiving all those people
who have wronged you."

'Man, I wanted to fall down with shock. How could
this guy have possibly known what I had said to God?
There was no way Marcus would have been able to tell
him a thing – I hadn't even *told* Marcus!

'Charles Slagle then pointed at me and said: "Receive
your healing in Jesus' name."'

Es paused for a moment. I knew that he was overwhelmed with the experience of it all.

'I began to shake and Marcus had to hold onto me.
My face was hot, but I knew, I really knew, that I was
going to be all right.'

I kept shaking my head in amazement at what Es was
saying. I knew that God had affected my life; I could
feel it in my heart. But believing that Jesus could heal Es
was something way beyond my understanding. I had
read about Jesus' healing people numerous times in the
Bible and I'd wondered, could it really happen today, in
my lifetime? Well, here was the proof, right in front of
me.

◆   ◆   ◆

'Hallelujah, I've seen the light!' A deep, loud voice bellowed out behind me as I was locking my car. I had just
finished a shift at Chimes. My boss wanted me to do
some 'backup' work at a club in Bow, east London. One

of the bouncers must have spotted me, hence the sarcastic remark.

Taking a deep breath, I sauntered towards the guys at the door. Heat surged up inside me and if I could, I would have jumped back in my car and gone home. I had to front it out.

I couldn't bring myself to find out who had shouted to me, but I looked a few of them in the eye and they couldn't hold my gaze.

Since his healing, Es was the number one spokesperson for God. Whether people wanted to hear what he had to say or not didn't matter – he was telling them, live and direct! I could fully understand why he was so excited at having his life turned around; after all, he'd been completely healed, and he had to let everyone know.

This put me under the spotlight as Es's story included me, and up until this point I hadn't been very vocal in telling people about Jesus. I wasn't ashamed to say I was a Christian; my reticence in letting people know was more to do with the fact that my life was not matching up – I couldn't 'talk the talk' if I wasn't 'walking the walk'. Some of the guys I worked with would rib me.

'So, you're a Bible-basher, eh, Ian?'

'Church on Sunday now?'

But even though people were laughing at me, which I found a bit annoying, it didn't deter me from being a Christian. And as Es was talking more and more about his new-found faith, I gained confidence as well.

Early one morning outside Chimes, Des approached me. 'Ian, can I have a word with you a minute?'

I thought he was going to ask if he could borrow some money. But what he actually said took me by surprise.

'Have you really become a Christian?' He seemed genuinely interested in what I had to say.

'Yeah.' My right hand momentarily clasped the knuckle-duster that was in my pocket. My left arm rested against the truncheon that was inside my jacket. I felt bad. How could I honestly say that I was a Christian when I had weapons on my person that could maim or cause death?

I told Des how I became a Christian and the effect that being a Christian was having on my life. I gave him the gospel. 'You should give your life to Jesus, Des.'

He grinned, shaking his head. 'No, I don't need him just yet.'

Driving home my head was a mess. I thanked God for the opportunity to tell Des about him, but I knew that my life could not continue the way it was. The very nature of door work was one of violence and aggression, and I had to have my weapons on me to use at a moment's notice. I wanted Jesus to take me out of the door work and bring along some other employment.

When I got home, I went into my bedroom and got my Bible. Flicking through the Psalms I stopped at 91: 'He will cover you with his feathers, and under his wings you will find refuge; his faithfulness will be your shield and rampart. You will not fear the terror of night' (vv. 4,5). The words jumped off the page at me. I knew that God was telling me that he would protect me – always. Now, I had to do my part and trust him. But how? I kept thinking that the easiest thing would be a new job. But I felt that that was not the way God was going to do it. I had to simply put those words I had just read into action, and believe – have faith – that what God's Word said was exactly what was going to happen.

Leaving for work that night, I nervously left the knuckle-duster and truncheon in my drawer. I felt naked. I realized that for years my confidence in taking care of myself and dealing with any situation had really been because I had these implements of violence in my pockets.

Each night as I went to work, I began to feel more and more certain of God's protection and defence of my life. Most nights were uneventful, which I felt was God's doing, letting me know that he was watching over me. But a few weeks later, my faith in God was challenged. The same guy who had spat in my face returned for his revenge.

As the punters came into Chimes, I spied this guy, raging, waving a large hammer, and issuing death threats.

'All my mates are laughing at me because of *you*.' He thrust the hammer out towards me. 'I'm the butt of everyone's joke 'cos of what you did to me. But not any more. I'm going to finish you off!' He smashed the hammer on the wall. I just looked at him, feeling somewhat detached and yet peaceful. I saw some of the other doormen heading for the side door. I knew the idea was to get behind the guy and sort him out. I shouted to them, 'No, get back, get back!' They stopped abruptly, turned and came back. This man did not know that I had saved him from a beating.

Calling out to the guy I asked him to put his hammer down. Our eyes locked as indecision flicked across his face. A few moments passed, and he dropped the hammer.

'Now, let's sort this out,' I said with more confidence than I felt. I knew that punters like this guy were unpredictable. But my new-found faith in God had got me this far, and I had to see it through. The guy walked towards me, calmly. The psyched-up, uncontrollable man of earlier moments had gone. Instead, a peaceful guy had taken his place. He approached me as I continued to talk to him.

'Look, mate, what happened the other night is history. Let's just forget it happened, and move on. All right, mate?' I stretched out my hand apprehensively. The guy took and shook it. He mumbled something and, bending to retrieve his hammer, turned and left.

My colleagues behind me were stunned. 'That's amazing,' said Des. 'I've never seen anything like it before. How did you manage to do that?'

I laughed. 'It's the power of God, Des. You should try it.'

This was firm confirmation to me that God always honours his word to anyone who dares to trust him.

◆   ◆   ◆

My hunger for God was increasing. I went to church with an eagerness to find out more about the God who was protecting me and my family. I was getting more comfortable being with God's people, and would join in worshipping and praising his name. But there was an ongoing problem that was causing me grief, and that was how I was obtaining my money. When I dropped my offering into the bag, to me it was tainted money not worthy to give to God. If I had given money that I had rightfully earned I would have felt clean and accepted. But it was with heaviness of heart that I was giving this stolen money.

'How can I earn enough to provide for me and my family?' I would regularly pray and cry out to God. I never got an answer. I just felt worse and worse. The fact was, the owner of Chimes was a bit of a drunk and he entrusted the money collected at the door to me. I would pocket the tips and money for the other guys. On top of my wages I was getting about £200 a week. How could I give that up, and how was I going to earn that much money?

Each week the bills would mount up and I would be engaged in a mental battle: How was I going to pay the rent? How was I going to buy food? How was I going to put petrol in my car? Even with the money I was stealing it seemed that I never, ever had enough to see us through the week. I wanted to get my money straight and clean.

God's answer was through his Word. I was reading the New Testament late one night when again a scripture loaded with a challenge leapt off the page and hit me hard: 'And my God will meet all your needs according to his glorious riches in Christ Jesus' (Phil. 4:19). I tussled with the thought of giving up my illegal dealings, but in the end I knew it was the only way forward.

My next shift at Chimes came round soon enough. As money was handed to me I lovingly handled each note, and placed it in the till. Usually by the middle of the shift my pockets would have been filled with some of these notes. Not tonight. Internally, I struggled with not helping myself to the money, but I was determined to break the stronghold that stealing had over me. I got through the night without taking a penny. The next night was the same.

When I got home, I laid my wages on the table in front of me and began to work out how much I needed to pay out. The scripture of God meeting my needs came zooming into my head.

'I believe you, Jesus,' I said. 'I know that you'll help me.'

How I got through the week was a mystery, but I successfully met all my bills for that week.

Once again God's Word had proven to be true. From that point on, God faithfully provided for me. I found that I always had enough money to see me through the week. When I was fiddling the door money, I was always broke; I couldn't make ends meet. Money was being sapped out of my life in various ways – the car would break down; the TV would conk out; I'd have a large gas bill . . . it was as though my pockets had holes in them. This changed when I straightened out my finances. God was there for me.

The last battle that I had to win was the drug-taking. Steroids had been in my life forever, it seemed. As my body got bigger, my muscles more prominent, so my dependency on steroids increased, enabling me to compete. From a Christian standpoint this was not good. Taking steroids for years had been damaging my health; my kidneys were impaired, and the gynaecomstia forced me to stop competing – which eventually stopped me taking steroids.

One day, Steve Jamison, a member of the church, invited Valerie and me to have lunch with his family.

'What was the worst thing about you before you became a Christian?' asked Steve. For a minute I paused. The violent acts and drug-taking went through my mind.

'Bodybuilding,' I said, with some conviction. As I spoke, it was like a new revelation to me. 'I always wanted to do something with my life, and when I got into bodybuilding, I thought I'd arrived. It completely took me over. I would eat, think and sleep bodybuilding. I would've given up everything to become a champion. My obsession with bodybuilding was such that it was god to me.' I surprised myself by what I said next. 'And do you know, Steve, if I had an opportunity to get rid of my gynaecomstia, I would never compete again.' I meant every word of it.

That was Sunday afternoon. On Monday morning, I was put to the test. A letter arrived from the hospital in Billericay to say that an appointment had been made available to me, on the National Health Service, to remove the gynaecomastia. I was shocked. I wasn't even aware that my name was on the waiting list.

Apparently, the surgeon who was going to perform the operation at the private hospital had put my name on the NHS list when I didn't turn up. I knew that Jesus was offering me a way out. With the letter in my hand, I prayed to the Lord, and thanked him. I also knew that I'd keep my promise – I would never compete again. My desire for bodybuilding had gone.

Becoming a Christian had changed my life and my focus. All my old ambitions and yearnings had slowly been chipped away. In their place was a hunger for the things of God; to pray, to read the Bible, to go to church. A new me was emerging. A new life was happening.

8

TOUGH TALK

One Sunday morning in January 1996, I watched as the worship team sang, the ushers served and various people kept the life of the church bubbling. And I cried out to God, 'What can I do?' I really wanted to do something meaningful for God, not only because he had done so much for me, but because of who he is.

Later that week, the leader of the church, Pastor Steve Derbyshire, called me.

'Ian,' he said, 'I would like you to give your testimony of how God has changed your life, and perhaps you could lift some weights as well?'

I was surprised. I did not see myself as a speaker, standing in front of lots of people, opening up my life to them. But I was more than happy to let others know about how God had worked in me. So, a few Sunday evenings later, I was given the opportunity to share my life story.

After I had performed some powerlifting demonstrations and told my story, several people, including an old lady, came forward when the congregation was asked if there was anyone who wanted to give their life to Jesus. I felt so encouraged by the way my story had affected this old lady, that I knew, given the chance, many more people could be similarly touched.

In March 1996 I was invited to speak at a church called The Powerhouse in Wood Green, north London. I took some guys with me to help out. When we arrived that evening, we noticed the church had put up some posters, advertising us. They called the evening 'Tough Talk'. The name stuck!

A few months later, I received a call from the chaplain of Highpoint Prison in Suffolk, asking if I could come and talk to some of the inmates about my experience with God. I called some of my mates, and off we went to Suffolk. Throughout the journey I was filled with trepidation at how the inmates would respond to us. I needn't have been concerned. It was very positive and, in fact, I was a bit amazed that these men – who would probably not have wanted to listen to anyone talking about God – were listening to us! The reception that we received reaffirmed in my heart and mind that this is what God wanted me to do.

♦ ♦ ♦

'I don't want to do door work any more, God,' I whispered to the Lord as I stood outside a bar in west London. I wanted out. It was the summer of 1996; European football was coming to London, and I realized this would impact hugely on all the pubs. I didn't want to be caught up in the maelstrom of violence that I knew would happen.

So I took a step of faith. I sent out letters to pubs in London and the surrounding areas.

ARE YOU PREPARING FOR THE EUROPEAN
FOOTBALL COMING TO LONDON?

ALL SENSIBLE MANAGERS AND LICENCEES NEED
TO TAKE EXTRA
SECURITY MEASURES.
CONTACT IAN McDOWALL AT
SOUTHERN COURT SECURITIES

I had no staff. I had no office base. I had no money. But what I did have was a trust and belief in God, that he would guide me in setting up my own company.

It was miraculous how God answered my prayers. By the time the football started, my new-found company was already providing security for fifteen pubs, with a staff of thirty! It seemed like an overnight success; I had gone from a bouncer to a businessman without any help from anyone. Everything I had accomplished was strictly by the hand of the Lord.

My life was now an open book. I could be honest and truthful with my wife, and not lie about where our money was coming from; I felt as if a huge weight had been lifted from my shoulders, as I really wanted us to be one, and not have any hidden agendas. By the end of that year, by the grace of God, we were able to buy our first house, which would have been unthinkable in the past.

As my business grew, I needed office space, as I was operating out of my home and it was not practical. My friend Tom was a barber who owned offices above his shop in South Woodford, Essex. I had been praying for somewhere to manage my business, and when I viewed the premises I knew it was just right. Valerie was the office manager, typing, answering the phone, sorting out all the paperwork, whilst I managed the men.

A friend of mine used to come to my office on a Tuesday evening, and we would pray, read the Bible and talk about God. I looked forward to this time together, as it was hard to attend midweek church meetings because of my business commitments. It wasn't long before a few other guys would come on Tuesdays, and together we fellowshipped. It was a precious time for each of us as we seemed to get to know each other and God in new and different ways.

In 1997 I could see that my business was expanding and I knew it was God's favour on my life. I hired more office staff to work alongside Valerie. I was employing more guys to fulfil the contracts that were coming in from clubs and pubs throughout London. I had some steady regulars who continually used my services, and it was in my interest to keep them sweet!

One such contract was for a pub in north London. The guy that owned it had a building business; he was a big man and really fancied himself. Early one evening I was visiting another contract in the West End, when this guy called me. He was irate, spewing profanities. His accent was thick and guttural and it was hard to understand him, but I managed to get all the bad words and the fact that one of my workers had not turned up at his bar. The man wouldn't listen to me. Instead, he shouted and ranted and raved. The phone clicked in my ear just as I was going to speak. My temper rose to a dangerous level.

'Right! I'm going to sort this bloke out once and for all.' I jumped into my car and manoeuvred myself through the busy London traffic.

I was livid. All thoughts of God, love, peace and joy were far from my mind. In slamming the phone down on me, this guy had dented my pride and I wanted him to pay. I bashed the steering wheel with my hand, and shouted at other drivers who cut me up, even though they couldn't hear me. My 'old self' reared its ugly head and I was in the mood for fighting. But as I got closer to the bar, I could feel myself 'coming down'. I began to pray and give the situation over to God. My anger abated and my head cleared. As I parked the car, I was still expecting a confrontation with the guy. So I approached the bar ready to handle whatever was going to happen.

To my relief, when I got inside my worker had turned up and the owner was nowhere in sight. I knew that as a man, my reaction to the guy was natural. If a man insults and goads another man, a verbal and physical confrontation is to be expected. But as a Christian, rolling around the pavement trying to beat someone's brains out was just not on . . .

This incident made me realize that I could no longer do this side of the job. I needed someone else, someone who was able to remain cool and keep order. One of my dependable doormen was called Martin. He was tough enough and had the respect of the other workers to be able to manage them.

During a Christian men's breakfast meeting I was sitting next to a big guy who engaged me in conversation, telling me about his life story. Looking at me he said, 'You look like you've done some training.'

I nodded. 'Yeah, I have.'

As we continued to talk I realized that this guy, who told me his name was Arthur, would be perfect to speak at one of the monthly meetings that I was doing in Highpoint Prison. So I asked him, and he came and spoke at our next meeting in the prison. Driving home with Arthur in the passenger seat of my car, I asked him if he would like to attend the prayer meeting that was held in my office on Tuesday evenings. He said he would.

The following Tuesday, Arthur walked into the meeting, suited and booted. He glanced around at us and sat down, fully participating. When the meeting was over, I noticed that he picked up one the 50,000 leaflets that I'd had printed for an event that I was planning in the Princes Theatre in Clacton-on-Sea, Essex.

In speaking publicly about my life experiences and how I became a Christian, I'd realized that there were many people who needed to know about Jesus and all that salvation entails – but most people don't attend church. As I had became more confident in the things of God, I'd found I wanted to tell others about him, so I'd reasoned to myself that I had to take the 'church' to people. With the Tough Talk team, not only did we want to talk about God and our lives, but we wanted to show people that we were *real*. Lifting weights, which is what we all did best, was a way in which this could be demonstrated.

Alongside managing my security business, I began to spend equal time managing Tough Talk. We as a group were being asked to speak at different venues through the UK. It was exciting to see people, total strangers, responding to the call of salvation. This is what caused me to initiate the meeting in Clacton.

My mum had moved to Clacton, and I was often there with my family, visiting her. I had spent time walking about and had thought that it would be a good place to have a Tough Talk meeting. So I'd contacted churches and various places, telling them about the coming event. I'd had posters made and placed around the seaside resort. I bought advertising space in the local newspapers and had some of the leaflets posted through the surrounding homes. The theatre held 1,000 people – I knew that God had led me to do this, as I knew that through my own volition I would never have taken on such a venture! I was a bit apprehensive about how many people would come, but I knew that it wasn't about numbers. I was more concerned that the people who came did so because they had a need that they knew could only be met by God.

The afternoon before the evening meeting in Clacton, me and the guys were down on the beach, lifting weights. A large crowd surrounded us; it was like a circus atmosphere by the sea. A coach-load of my friends from my church in Ilford had come to support us. They gave out leaflets about the evening meeting, and chatted to people who wanted to know what was going on.

Arriving at the theatre that evening, I could see large numbers of people were streaming into it. Arthur and his wife, Jacqui, were waiting just outside as I approached the doors. Jacqui laid her hand on my shoulder, and began to quietly pray for me. Arthur looked a bit anxious, and butterflies were fluttering in my stomach, but a calm confidence began to still my mind, and I felt reassured that God was in control.

The meeting was fantastic. The people responded overwhelmingly, which helped confirm to me that I was going in the right direction. Many responded to the gospel message, and we gave out packages that had gospel booklets and leaflets to help them understand the commitment that they had made.

As I listened to Arthur's testimony, I realized that he was perfect for Tough Talk, and that our lives would be meshed together.

By the year 2000, Tough Talk was speaking at over three hundred meetings a year, which was by invitation alone – none of our work was self-promoting in any way. It was continual evidence that God was using Tough Talk to bring hope to people's lives.

It was apparent to me that we now needed more structured plans. Arthur formed Tough Talk into a charitable trust, which increased our credibility. Predominately, we were doing more and more meetings in prisons.

The format of our meetings was (and is) a simple one: We'd take over the prison gym; all the weights were set out. About a hundred inmates would march in and sit on wooden benches, listen to us speak and partake in the meetings. Today, we get hundreds of letters from inmates telling us how we have impacted their lives, through our meetings and books.

After one such meeting in a prison, a young guy came up to me, angry, with clenched fists. He shoved his face into mine.

'Are you for real?'

'If I am for real,' I said, coolly, 'what are you going to do about it?' As the words left my mouth, I wondered if my response was a bit heavy.

About a month later we received a letter from this same inmate. He told us that in returning to his cell, he thought about what we had said about Jesus during the meeting. He apologized to me and said that he'd asked God to forgive him, and asked Jesus into his life. He continued that almost instantly, he was filled with a peace that he had never experienced before; it was something outside of himself. He and another inmate were getting baptized as a result of that one meeting.

◆　◆　◆

My business had grown by 2001, and I was able to delegate work to my employees that afforded me time to work for Tough Talk. Arthur was now a full-time worker for the charity, and together we were able to do more meetings.

Tough Talk was becoming better known, and during 2003, and for the next few years, we were interviewed by the BBC, Sky TV and radio stations. Our book, telling our life stories, was being read by many people.

My daughter, Bianca, left home to go to Birmingham University in 2007. Valerie and I dropped her off at her lodgings just outside the university. There were tears in my eyes as I marvelled at the fact that if we had not become Christians, and I had continued my previous style of living, there was no way that my daughter would have grown up in a stable home, with responsible parents that encouraged her to reach her full potential. I thanked God for being in our lives to enable us to prosper and do well.

Tough Talk is still very much in demand. Since 2009, Arthur and I tend mainly to speak in prisons throughout England, Scotland and Wales; we give our testimony in about a hundred per year. The rest of the Tough Talk team speak in churches, youth clubs and schools.

Never in a million years would I, or anyone who knew me in my younger, wilder days, believe that I would own my own business, have a wife, daughter and son in a secure, loving family unit, and be travelling the UK and other parts of the world talking about Jesus. I know for sure that it is in giving my life to Jesus that my life and the lives of my loved ones have been turned completely around for good.

The Bible says that when a person gives their life to Jesus, old things (their past) have gone away; everything becomes new (see 2 Cor. 5:17). This is so true for me. My life was unrecognizable, just a short time after I became a Christian. The greatest change was having inner peace. No longer was insomnia my bedfellow. When I faced trials and tribulations, anxiety would attack me; but once I began to pray and trust Jesus for the outcome, I was at peace again.

I used to say that Christians were wimps and fairies, and used Christianity as a crutch to escape the realities of life. Now I know that even though it's good to have physical strength for everyday life, what's really needed to make you stronger is inner strength – which can only come from God.

EPILOGUE

You have now read both of our stories. The question we would like to put to you is this: Are we telling the truth?

If you believe we are telling the truth – that our stories of how Jesus Christ has changed our lives are real – then the gospel, the good news about Jesus, must be true. The gospel of God's Son is for everybody. No matter how bad or how good you are, we all make mistakes before God. Jesus said, 'anyone who says, "You fool!" will be in danger of the fire of hell' (Matt. 5:22). God's standards are different to ours. There is a way that seems right to humankind, yet that way leads to death (see Prov. 14:12). '. . . the wages of sin is death, but the gift of God is eternal life' (Rom. 6:23). This is the good news:

> For God so loved the world that he gave his one and only Son, that whoever believes in him shall not perish but have eternal life.
>
> (John 3:16)

If you feel this is for you, here is a simple prayer you can say:

Dear Lord Jesus, I am sorry for the wrong things I have done in my life.

I believe that you, Lord Jesus, died on the cross for me, and took away all my sins. I believe that you rose from the dead, and are alive today. Please forgive me, Jesus, and come into my life.

Thank you, Jesus.

Amen.

If you would like to know more about Jesus, please feel free to contact our office by email or letter. It would be great to hear from you.

If you are a church or Christian organization or prison and would like to book Tough Talk for a meeting, our details are below.

From all the team at Tough Talk, we do truly pray that God will bless you.

Tough Talk
119 George Lane,
South Woodford,
London,
E18 1AN

Email: tough-talk@ntlworld.com
Phone: 0208 923 6190
Website: www.tough-talk.com

Tough Talk 2

More Life-Changing Stories from the Tough Talk Team

with
Millie Murray

Joe Lampshire – '"YOU WILL DIE" . . . Playing the Ouija board was just for a laugh; I had done it many times before. But this was something way, way out of my experience and it wasn't funny.' For Joe, this was just the beginning of a long battle with the spirit world. As dark forces threatened to claim Joe's life, could light ever break through?

Martyn Parrish – 'It was heady stuff and, of course, I wanted to do it again. I wanted to drop some pills and then ride my bike. This was living! Or so I thought.' At first the drugs freed Martyn's mind, and then they began to completely take over. As heroin became Martyn's closest and most destructive friend, could he ever find peace?

Simon Pinchbeck – 'I'd been greedy, thinking how much I'd make out of my investment, and now it was gone. I felt the need to settle the matter, preferably by slowly killing each man involved.' A hunger for money and involvement with tough and violent police corps had sent Simon's life spiralling out of control. Deserted by friends and in huge debt, would he ever find a way out?

978-1-86024-700-2

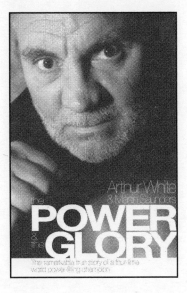

Power & the Glory

*The Remarkable Story of
a Four-Time World
Powerlifting Champion*

*Arthur White &
Martin Saunders*

Arthur White had it all. Not only was he a successful businessman and happy family man, but as a champion powerlifter, he was literally on top of the world. But when he got to the top, he wasn't satisfied . . .

As he searched for a greater high, Arthur's life spiralled out of control. Drug addiction, an intense affair and a descent into violence followed, and before long death seemed like the only way out. As he stared into the abyss, an incredible encounter turned Arthur's life upside down. He would never be the same again . . .

978-1-86024-560-2

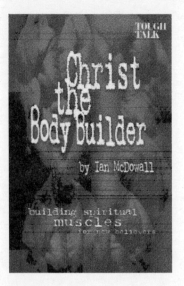

Christ the Body Builder

Building Spiritual Muscles for New Believers

Ian McDowall

Christ the Body Builder is an introduction to the Christian faith written by Tough Talk team member and former bodybuilder Ian McDowall. Using illustrations from the world of bodybuilding, Ian provides a solid grounding in the vital Christian disciplines in a warm, conversational and very readable style. Includes photographs of the Tough Talk team in action.

978-1-85078-478-0

DVDs

Tough Talk

True Life Stories

This DVD tells the incredible stories of Arthur White, Steve Johnson, Ian McDowall and Marcus Williams. Each has a powerful story of how God rescued them from lives of violence, drug abuse and alcoholism.

5028981021550

Tough Talk

Stories From the Front Line

Members of the Tough Talk team discuss candidly the topics of pornography, addiction, anger and forgiveness.

The guys don't pretend to have all the answers but talk openly and honestly of their own battles with these issues.

The short study guide which comes in the pack provides material for group discussion on each of the topics.

5014182055197